In Search of The Third Man

In Search of
The Third Man

CHARLES DRAZIN

Limelight Editions

First Limelight Edition July 2000

Copyright © 1999 Charles Drazin

All right reserved under International and Pan-American Copyright Conventions.

Published in the United States by Proscenium Publishers Inc., New York,
by arrangement with Methuen Publishing Limited, London.

Library of Congress Cataloging-in-Publication Data

Drazin, Charles, 1960-
In search of the Third man / Charles Drazin.-- 1st Limelight ed.
p. cm.
Originally published: Methuen, 1999.
Includes bibliographical references.
ISBN 0-87910-294-2
1. Third man (Motion picture) I. Title.

PN1997.T42873 D73 2000
791.43'72--dc21

00-025226

For Dinah

Contents

Contents

Acknowledgements

I'd like to thank the following for their help in the course of writing this book: Noreen Best, Gordon Brook-Shepherd, Kevin Brownlow, Jerome Chodorov, Bob Dunbar, David Eady, Michael Earley, Bill Fairchild, Roy Fowler, Bill Hamilton, Guy and Kerima Hamilton, John Hawkesworth, Christian Hermansen, Robin Lowe, Martin McLean, Elizabeth Montagu, Laura Morris, Saffron Parker, Donna Poppy, Max Reed, David Russell, Jilly St James, David Salmo, Michael Shelden, Roger Smither, Henry Smithson, Norman Spencer, Brigitte Timmermann and Carol Walker.

Indispensable providers of documentary information were the David O. Selznick Collection, Harry Ransom Humanities Research Center, the University of Texas at Austin; and the special collections of the British Film Institute Library. Indispensable providers of books – and somewhere to work – were the British Library and the London Library.

I am grateful to the following for permission to reproduce photographs: AKG London, the British Film Institute, Canal + Image UK, Hulton Getty, Österreichisches Institut für Zeitgeschichte; and to Orion Books for permission to reproduce the map on p. x.

Every effort has been made to trace and contact copyright holders before publication. If notified, I undertake to rectify errors or omissions at the earliest opportunity.

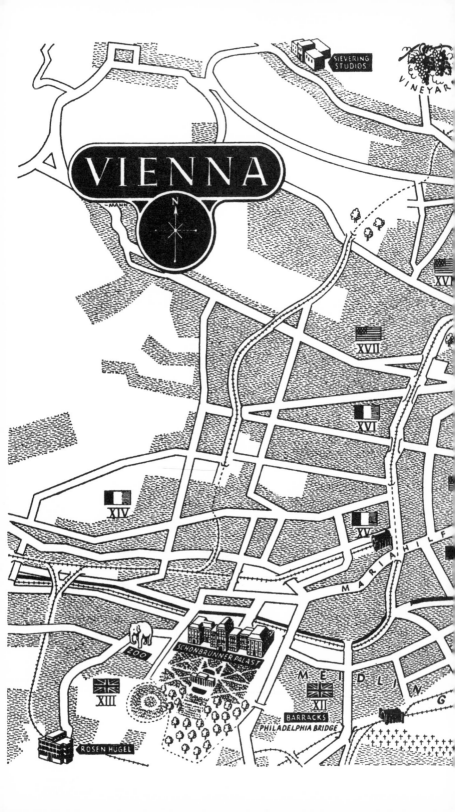

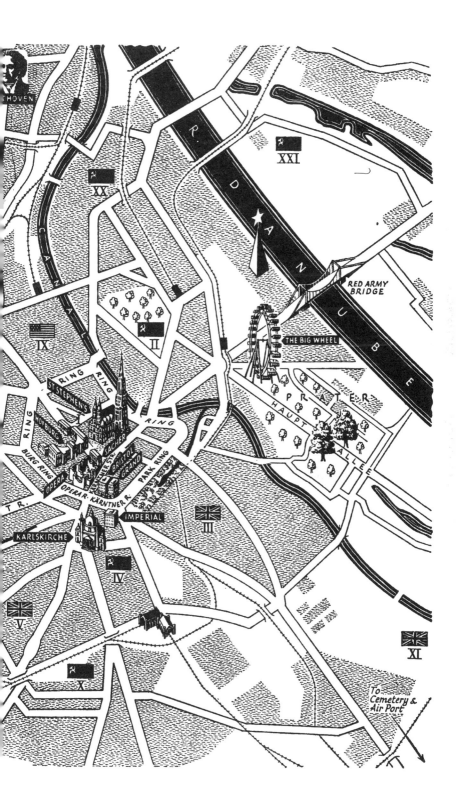

Preface

This story begins with a writer checking into a hotel room in Vienna with an idea for a film. He spends two weeks in the city soaking in the atmosphere and doing some research. He then travels on to Italy and over the next few weeks writes a treatment in the form of a short novel.

Back in England the film impresario who commissioned him is delighted with his work and puts together a deal with a Hollywood producer. In the months that follow the individuals who devote themselves to this project that started with just one man multiply like cells dividing under a microscope. A director works closely with the writer to produce a script, and other writers are brought in. The stars and supporting players are hired, while the script, in its various stages, is passed on to an art director, a cameraman, an associate producer, an editor, a production manager and so on. Eight thousand miles away, the Hollywood producer follows progress closely and, in consultation with his own sizeable team of helpers, makes many suggestions.

In the process of collaboration, the original story changes and takes on a new form, like an embryo becoming distinct from the cluster of cells out of which it first grew. Although it is certainly possible to single out this or that individual for the particular importance of his or her contribution, if we are to be honest, the film has not one but several authors. Even this scarcely does justice to the full complexity. For the final film turns out not as any of its individual contributors had planned, but according to the interaction – or aggregate – of their egos, and according to countless other circumstances beyond anyone's control. A vital ingredient is accident, arranging the conjunction of personalities and events as to make the difference between the run-of-the-mill – which many other film versions of the writer's work had been – and the truly extraordinary. This book is about one of my favourite films, *The Third Man*, it is about how individuals work together – or often don't work together – and it is about chance. If it has any moral it is no more than what the film itself reveals so stylishly – that things are rarely as they seem.

The 1950 Academy Award ceremony serves as an example. *The Third Man* made a surprisingly poor showing. It received only three nominations – for best direction, best black-and-white photography and best editing. A lengthy dispute between Sir Alexander Korda and David Selznick had delayed its American release by several months and denied it that essential prerequisite of Oscar success – then as now – an effective publicity campaign.

In the event only the cameraman Robert Krasker won an Oscar. Although his award was as fully deserved as these things ever can be, it was not his achievement alone. Perhaps the two most celebrated sequences in the film – Orson Welles' first appearance in a Viennese doorway and the ending, in which Alida Valli walks past the waiting Joseph Cotten – were shot by other cameramen, John Wilcox and Hans Schneeberger (the latter – the ex-lover of Leni Riefenstahl – remained completely un-credited). Krasker was further helped to the award by – just to mention a very few people – the flawless art direction of Vincent Korda; the editing of Oswald Hafenrichter, which invested the images with such dramatic weight; and the direction of the cinema's greatest orchestrator of chance, Carol Reed.

Perhaps no other film better illustrates the hidden alchemy of the cinema, but finally this book is simply a tribute to one of the most loved and enduring of British films on its fiftieth birthday. Many happy returns to *The Third Man*.

1

'Mixing Fact with Fiction'

'Can I ask, is Mr Martins engaged in a new book?'
'Yes. It's called *The Third Man*.'
'A novel, Mr Martins?'
'It's a murder story. I've just started it. It's based on fact.'
'Are you a slow writer, Mr Martins?'
'Not when I get interested.'
'I'd say you were doing something pretty dangerous this
     time.'
'Yes?'
'Mixing fact with fiction.'

Graham Greene gave an account of the origins of *The Third Man* in his memoirs and in a preface to the published story, but it would be foolish to take these any more at face value than Harry Lime's 'fatal' accident in the film. Mixing fact with fiction was as much a characteristic in Greene's various accounts of his own life as it was in his film scripts or novels.

According to Greene, it was Sir Alexander Korda who first had the idea to make a film set against the background of the Four Power occupation of Vienna. He had wanted Greene to collaborate a second time with the director Carol Reed after their successful partnership on *The Fallen Idol*. But all Greene had in response to Korda's original initiative was this sentence, which he had written several years previously: 'I had paid my last farewell to Harry a week ago, when his coffin was lowered into the frozen February ground, so that it was with incredulity that I saw him pass by, without a sign of recognition, among the host of strangers in the Strand.'[1]

His first step, he recalled, was to visit Vienna, where he stayed for two weeks, doing research. Days went by, and nothing came to him. Then, on the day before he was to leave, everything fell into place when he had lunch with a British Intelligence officer. The officer told him about the 'Underground Police' who patrolled the city's enormous system of sewers, and the black market trade in adulterated penicillin, and at last he had his story.

But the surviving documents and personal recollections suggest a very different, less clear-cut version of events. *The Third Man* really owed its genesis to the initiatives of several people and the conjunction of several different circumstances.

Greene finished working on the script of *The Fallen Idol* (originally called *The Lost Illusion*) in the summer of 1947. He then focused his energies on finishing his novel *The Heart of the Matter*. On 27 September, as we know from his correspondence with his lover Catherine Walston, he sent the completed manuscript to his publisher, Heinemann. 'I have no ideas for another book and feel I never shall,' he confided. 'I feel very empty and played out.'[2] But two days later he wrote to her again. This time he was jubilant:

> I believe I've got a *book* coming. I feel so excited that
> I spell out your name in full carefully sticking my
> tongue between my teeth to pronounce it right. The
> act of creation is awfully odd and inexplicable, like
> falling in love ... Tonight I had a solitary good
> dinner where I usually go with My Girl and
> afterwards felt vaguely restless (not sexually, just
> restless) so I walked to the Café Royal and sat and
> read *The Aran Islands*, and drank beer till about 10
> and then I still felt restless, so I walked all up
> Piccadilly and back and went into a Gent's in Brick
> Street, and suddenly in the Gent's, I saw the three
> chunks, the beginning, the middle and the end, and
> in some ways all the ideas I had – the first sentence
> of the thriller about the dead Harry who wasn't dead,

the Risen-from-the-dead story, and then the other day
in the train all seemed to come together. I hope to
God it lasts – they don't always.

If Greene's account of thinking up the risen-from-the-dead
story seems rather like a resurrection itself, certainly it was a
theme which went back to his earliest years as a writer. In the
short story 'The Second Death', written in 1929, a dying and
dissolute man is haunted by the thought that he has died once
before. A friend tries to reassure him that this first death must
have been just a dream, but to little avail: ' "Old man," he said,
"suppose it was true. Suppose I had been dead. I believed it
then, you know ... I went straight for a couple of years. I
thought it might be a sort of second chance ..." ' The voice
belongs to a kind of repentant Harry Lime that we never see in
the movie. In Greene's *Ministry of Fear* (1943) a group of Nazi
conspirators feign the death of one of their number, a Mr
Cost, and pin his 'murder' on the hero, Arthur Rowe, in order
to scare him out of his investigation. Later Rowe bumps into
Cost still very much alive. This sort of resurrection was much
more Harry's style.

While Greene rejoiced over his story about 'the dead Harry
who wasn't dead', Carol Reed that autumn was on the floor at
Shepperton Studios shooting *The Lost Illusion*. It had been
adapted from Greene's short story 'The Basement Room' and
would open the following year as *The Fallen Idol*. Reed was
finding it tough-going, remembered Guy Hamilton who was
his assistant director on the film. The child star, Bobby
Henrey, was proving difficult to direct, and, in his efforts to
draw out a halfway decent performance, Reed was falling far
behind schedule. He feared that the film, which depended so
heavily on Henrey, would be a disaster, and he worried about
the implications for the future. 'I think we're in trouble,' he
confided to Hamilton. 'We may have to make a comedy
thriller.' The great advantage of the comedy thriller, he
explained, was that 'you're not walking a tightrope ... you

miss some of the laughs, you miss some of the thrills but hopefully there's something left'.[3] Hitchcock stayed out of trouble by making them all the time.

So, late in 1947 Reed approached Greene, with whom he had worked very happily on the script of *The Lost Illusion*, and asked him if he had any suitable ideas for that most dependable of genres, the comedy thriller. Greene then told him about the dead Harry, and the two went off to see Korda. At this point Greene had not just the first sentence of his story, but also the beginning, middle and end. He had intended it as a novel, but doubtless the considerable sum he could expect out of another film assignment would have encouraged him to be flexible. Korda liked the idea but suggested a change of setting.

After the war Sir Alexander Korda was keen that his company London Film Productions should establish links with the former occupied or enemy territories on the Continent. For many years these countries had been without British or American films, and Korda saw an opportunity to make a substantial profit by promoting his old productions. But strict currency controls throughout Europe made it difficult to remit the earnings back to Britain.

The practical solution was to put these revenues to some constructive purpose in the countries in which they were generated. Korda, who had in his time produced films in Budapest, Berlin, Paris and not least Vienna, and whose London Film Productions had had offices all over Europe, was perhaps better placed than any other British producer to take advantage of the situation. Indeed, *The Third Man* was just the first of a series of films that he would make with the help of the foreign currency generated from the screening of his films abroad. In the same year, for example, *The Wooden Horse* would be shot on a budget made up of an equal amount of English pounds and German marks, while Launder and Gilliatt's *State Secret* would draw heavily on Korda's reserves of Austrian schillings and Italian lire. All these transactions had to be approved by the Bank of England, which in those days, before the Euro, played a pivotal if totally un-chronicled role in British film production.

In December 1947 – perhaps slightly before his meeting with Greene and Reed – Korda had sent his assistant, Elizabeth Montagu, on a tour of Europe to report on the state of his old offices and their future commercial potential. 'I wrote and telephoned reports to Korda as often as I could,' remembered Montagu. 'I was updating him on practically everything, because nobody knew a thing in those days. I'm sure the descriptions I wrote and the things I said to Korda about Central Europe, about Prague and Vienna, made him realise that this is another world, and in a way a very filmic one. And I think that probably sparked off his imagination.'[4] Korda had already shown an interest in Vienna as a setting for a film – back in 1938 he had commissioned Carl Zuckmayer (co-writer of *The Blue Angel*) to write a script about Imperial Austria – and he would naturally have been predisposed to ideas about a country where he had spent many of his formative years as a film-maker.

But Korda had quite a few offices in Europe – not least in Italy – and the evidence suggests that he mentioned not only Vienna as a possible setting for Greene's story but Rome too. In a letter agreement dated 26 January 1948 London Film Productions set out the terms of Greene's assignment.[5] He was to write 'an original story suitable for the production of a cinematograph film'. In pursuit of this he was 'to go to Vienna for approximately three weeks and from there to Italy for approximately eight weeks ... for the purpose of research work.' He would be paid £1000 plus expenses for a first treatment (about £20,000 in today's money), and then, if the company decided to go ahead, a further £3000 for a full treatment of about thirty thousand words. The project was described as 'an original post-war continental story to be based on either or both of the following territories: Vienna, Rome'. This was as precise as anyone seemed able to be at this stage. Greene may have had his beginning, middle and end when he and Reed first talked about the Harry idea, but Korda's brief to set the story against the background of post-war Europe would have necessitated a major rethink.

Greene flew out to Vienna on 11 February 1948. Elizabeth Montagu met him at the airport and booked him into the Sacher Hotel. She already knew to expect a far from straightforward character. Her first contact with him had been a cable from England giving the time and date of his arrival. It included instructions that she should send his wife a telegram signed in his name. 'It said something like, "So sorry I couldn't contact you before I left, but everything's fine here, etc etc." I said to him, "You lied because you weren't here." "Yes, I was in Brighton with my girlfriend and I didn't want my wife to know." '

Happy to implicate Elizabeth Montagu in his deceit, he seemed to enjoy the intrigue and the skulduggery, putting her in a spot. 'Everything he did was rather charming and rather unusual,' she remembered, and he had 'a wonderful sense of humour, ironic, unexpected', but his initial subterfuge seemed to set the tone of their time together.

She showed him around Vienna, which he didn't know. 'I took him everywhere. I took him to the ruins, I took him to places still standing, I took him everywhere you can think of, including the Great Wheel and all that. He became absolutely enamoured of Vienna.'

He was particularly drawn to its seamier side. Montagu remembered that he would ask her to come out with him in the evenings. 'We would go to the most terrible nightclubs – they were actually quite clearly brothels. And we'd sit in a box and watch a lot of alarmingly skinny ladies dancing around naked on the stage. I watched his reaction to this awful place ... and saw that he was clearly fascinated by it all. I remember asking him how he could equate his religious principles with sitting in a brothel getting drunk. And I remember, too, how convincingly he replied, and how brilliantly he equivocated on every point until he nearly succeeded in convincing me. But by that time we were probably both a little tipsy.'

When Greene first arrived in Vienna, he told Elizabeth Montagu that 'he didn't know what he was going to write, he hadn't the faintest idea'. He joked about it. So she did all she could to help spark off some ideas. She introduced him to the British military officials and the correspondents of the leading English newspapers. 'I thought they could brief him up on any questions because they were on the spot, they'd been on the spot for ages, and they knew all the details of things which I wouldn't know about, how much the rations were and all that sort of thing.'

Of course Greene certainly had some idea of what he was going to write, even if he was going to have to change his story about Harry considerably. But there was no reason why he should tell Elizabeth Montagu that.

She was particularly keen that Greene should meet Peter Smollett, the correspondent of *The Times*. Before Greene had come out to Vienna, she had talked to Smollett about some stories he had written on contemporary Vienna. She thought that Greene might be interested in them, since they provided ideal background. Smollett for his part hoped that Greene might be able to give him some advice about finding a publisher.

Elizabeth Montagu gave Greene the stories soon after his arrival. He read them in an evening, met Smollett and said that he would do what he could to help. As she could remember no notable reaction from Greene of any kind, Elizabeth Montagu was surprised a few months later to discover that the script had drawn heavily on the situations and background detail of one of the Smollett stories. 'I remember it had something to do – I remember this because I was so shocked by it – with a children's hospital and diluted antibiotics.' She was upset that Smollett's contribution had not been acknowledged, and again she felt implicated in a piece of low behaviour, having given Smollett the understanding that Greene would help him find a publisher for the stories.

But the evidence suggests there was nothing underhand in Greene's conduct, and that in the end Greene did help

Smollett even if it was not to get his stories published. For in June 1948 Smollett was duly hired by London Film Productions to give 'advice on the film script at present entitled *The Third Man* and to provide assistance in Vienna in connection with the production of a film to be based there'.[6] His fee was 200 guineas, which was probably a good deal more than most publishers of the time would have been prepared to offer for a book of short stories by an unknown writer. 'You will render your services hereunder to the best of your skill and ability,' stipulated Smollett's letter agreement, 'and shall collaborate in the writing of the said script with Mr Carol Reed and such other persons as the Company may require'. Under the agreement he was required to yield the complete copyright in any contributions he made to the script, but it was a standard and necessary clause, since London Films often employed additional writers to work on scripts. Korda understood the importance of getting a script right, and saw to it that they were worked and polished with a thoroughness that makes much of British cinema today seem decidedly amateur.

Besides Smollett there were two other un-credited writers who worked on *The Third Man* – Mabbie Poole, the wife of the playwright Rodney Ackland, and the American screenwriter Jerome Chodorov. And perhaps there were others that we don't know about. All would have had to agree to relinquish their copyright, and wouldn't have thought twice about it. The work they did was in practice like that of a publisher's editor, improving and polishing what was in substance another person's work.

It should also be added that Smollett asked Greene's literary agents, Pearn, Pollinger & Higham, to look after the negotiations with London Film Productions for him. His conduct was not one of a man who thought he had been hard done by. His correspondence in the London Film Productions files suggests an attitude of cheerful cooperation. Returning his signed contract on 21 September 1948, he added this postscript to his covering note: 'By the way, what is the position about "The Third Man"? Is he coming to Vienna this autumn and do you want me to have anything to do with him? I should be glad of a little advance notice of your intentions so as to be able to reserve time for him in my winter programme.'[7]

But even if Greene was innocent of duplicity on this particular occasion, it was some measure of him that Montagu should none the less have felt that he was up to some trickery. The reminiscences of Montagu and others suggest something fundamentally unreliable about Greene. He derived glee from mischief for its own sake, and spun fantasies that – like the man in Havana – you would be foolish to believe. If you're in the company of such a person you tag along with him for the fun and adventure, but learn to take what he has to say with a pinch of salt.

2

'Bombed About a Bit'

Austria recovered slowly from the privations of war. In the summer of 1946, after more than a year of peace, its citizens had to live on a diet of 1200 calories a day. This amounted to 'slow starvation', a visiting Select Committee of the British Parliament reported, and the situation was 'critical'. Nowhere was the country's devastation more apparent than in its capital, Vienna.

We can get an idea of what Greene would have found from the newspaper reports of the time, in which the faded and fallen city offered as regular and sad a spectacle as Beirut or Sarajevo would to a later generation.

'In other capitals of Europe there is either food or enthusiasm,' reported *The Times* in a special feature on the city. 'In Vienna one finds too little of either and sees less of the phoenix than of the ashes.' In a long, reflective piece a picture was built up of a vanquished and shamed people:

> The sun disguises the traces of hunger which appear
> in the slowness with which people move about and
> go up stairs ... It might matter less that the
> population have so little to eat if they themselves
> were devoured by some passion to rebuild, to start
> again. They still have to lift themselves through a
> spiritual as well as material wreckage. Their double
> past, the alluring Empire, and the domineering Reich,
> both collapsed within a lifetime, lie heavy on them,
> and everywhere one is reminded of it ... The
> charming gold pavilions of the Prater are wrecked,

and charred tanks still lie on their sides along the avenue. Four forlorn pleasure-cars have been hanging on the Giant Wheel for months, but still it has not begun to turn.[1]

In *The Third Man* of course the Great Wheel does turn, but haltingly, as if it too has been starved into slowness. Two years on, the film would revisit the physical and moral landscape that *The Times* had mapped out. The Wheel carries Holly Martins and Harry Lime high above the city. Lime looks down at the people, now tiny dots below. 'Would you really feel any pity if one of those dots stopped moving for ever?' he asks his old school friend. 'If I offered you twenty thousand pounds for every dot that stops, would you really, old man, tell me to keep my money – or would you calculate how many dots you could afford to spend?'

Austria itself had made a Faustian pact in its Anschsluss with Germany in 1938. Seven years later the country lay in ruins. In the last days of the war, the Red Army drove units of the SS out of central Vienna into the Prater. The amusement park was virtually levelled to the ground as a fierce battle raged. The only thing by some miracle to escape the destruction was the Great Wheel – as if the retreating SS had left it for Harry Lime, on the run himself. In the immediate aftermath of the war there were few better places than Vienna to understand the allure of evil, as well as the price that might be paid for succumbing to its temptation.

The scarred Great Wheel, rising above the burnt-out amusement park, must have seemed, to the few people who wandered that way, like an emblem of the city's folly – a city of delusion and disappointed dreams. Like some vast ground plan of itself, it found its echo in the Ringstrasse, the majestic boulevard that encircled the city. On Christmas Eve 1857 Emperor Franz Jozef ordered the old walls of Vienna to be pulled down, and the building in their place of a circle of great monuments, in glorification of the Habsburg Empire. These works, all built on a massive scale, included the Opera and the

Burgtheater, a town hall and parliament building, and, as Jan Morris put it, 'a university more utterly academic than Heidelberg, Cambridge and Salamanca put together, museums as overwhelmingly museumy as museums could possibly be, and all appearing to curve deferentially, even obsequiously, around the immense pillared and rambling sprawl of the Hofburg.'[2]

The sheer presumption of the scheme reminds one of the monuments that the fascists would erect half a century later. Adolf Hitler was an admirer. In *Mein Kampf* he wrote of his days in Vienna: 'From morning until late at night, I ran from one object of interest to another, but it was always the buildings that held my primary interest. For hours I could stand in front of the Opera, for hours I could gaze at the parliament; the whole Ring-Boulevard seemed to me like an enchantment out of *The Thousand and One Nights*.'

But if the Ringstrasse began as a magnificent fantasy of the nineteenth century, it ended as a grotesque absurdity of the twentieth. By an irony the last major structure would be completed in 1913, just in time to see the centuries-old Empire come tumbling down in the Great War. Out of the ruins emerged an impoverished republic, shorn of its dominion. The French statesman Clemenceau dubbed this rump of empire 'ce qui reste'. Vienna at its heart, a huge city built to rule over an Empire of 50 million and now at the disposal of a small country of only 7 million, had become the oversized head of a dwarf.

In the twentieth century Vienna would outdo itself in paradox. At the start of the century it was one of the world's great cosmopolitan cities, capital of the Habsburg Empire which had endured for over 600 years. Famed for its internationalism, it was a city where nationalities lived peacefully together and outsiders were welcomed. The citizens of Vienna were as likely to be Croat or Czech or Slovenian as Germanic. Many of them would have had relatives in Budapest or Prague or Trieste. Long before the Iron Curtain had been thought of, these were familiar cities that must have seemed as easy to visit as Manchester or Bristol for a Londoner. Then there were the Jews – some 200,000 of them in the city at the beginning of the war: they included doctors and lawyers and writers. They gave the place much of its charm and sophistication. Their number famously included Freud and Wittgenstein and Mahler and Schnitzler. And even that most Viennese of all composers, Johann Strauss, had a Jewish great-grandfather. Here was the epitome of the civilised metropolis that could inspire great artists. Then there was 'Red Vienna'. In the aftermath of the First World War the socialist rulers of the city pioneered communal housing projects and welfare programmes that turned Vienna into an example to the world of enlightened social progress. Yet this was the city which also nurtured the great scourge of civilisations. 'Vienna was and remained for me the hardest but also the most thorough school of my life,' wrote Hitler in *Mein Kampf*. 'In that city I received the basis of a view of life in general and a political way of looking at things in particular which later on I had only to supplement in single instances, but which never again deserted me.'

Jewel of fabled Mitteleuropa and beacon of socialism; inspiration to fascists and hotbed of racism. In having been these things, perhaps Vienna was simply remaining true to the symbol of the Habsburgs, the double-headed eagle that looked two ways. The real marvel was the speed with which it could switch from one to the other now that the old empire had gone: imperial capital, showcase of international socialism, city of the Third Reich, all within a single generation. In his recent history of Austria Gordon Brook-Shepherd tells the story of a man who during Vienna's celebrations of the Anschluss set off from home with a gun to assassinate Hitler. But as he pushed his way through the jubilant crowds, he wondered what was the point and turned back home.[3] Like sudden rain on a sunny day, the mood had turned and he'd been caught out.

When the victorious – although in the circumstances this doesn't seem quite the right word – German troops marched from the German frontier to Vienna, Austria's Cardinal

Theodore Innitzer ordered the churches to ring their bells in celebration and to unfurl swastika flags from their towers. Seven years later he would celebrate a thanksgiving mass for Germany's surrender. When British troops marched into Linz, they were greeted by a choir dressed in Hitler Youth uniform singing 'God Save the King'.[4] And during this *septennat*, at the request of the city authorities, the cobbles to repair the picturesque streets of Old Vienna came from Mauthausen concentration camp.[5] Such were the volte-faces possible in the land of the double-headed eagle.

In the plebiscite held a few days after the Anschluss, 99.75 per cent of the voters supported the union with Nazi Germany (although the Jews of course were not allowed to vote). *Bella gerant alii, tu felix Austria nube*, ran the old Habsburg saying. 'Let other people wage wars, while you, lucky Austria, marry.' But this time she had chosen the worst possible suitor, the very father of battles. The inevitable divorce challenged even Austria's ability to look both ways. In the last few months of the war Vienna would be bombed by the Americans, besieged by the Russians and shelled by the retreating Germans.

The statistics reveal what its peculiar fate – to be stuck in the middle – meant in practice. More than 8,000 buildings were completely destroyed, and another 40,000 damaged, altogether 28 per cent of the entire building stock in Vienna. 12.3 per cent of the city's dwellings had become uninhabitable. 270,000 people were made homeless. Not even the dead were allowed to rest in peace: 536 bombs fell on the Central Cemetery, where Harry Lime would be buried.[6]

In the city centre the rubble was many feet high. The bombsites included familiar names on every tourist's list of attractions – the Opera, the Burgtheater, St Stephen's Cathedral. It was the task of years to repair such devastation.

Everywhere Graham Greene would have walked that February of 1948, he would have seen the jagged, cavernous shells of buildings, chain-gangs of people passing stones, carts piled high with rubble. What he saw, we see in the film. The ruins provide a constant backdrop. Among the buildings destroyed – in an American air raid – was the Philipp-Hof, on the Albertinaplatz. It was situated just across from the Café Mozart, where Holly Martins meets Baron Kurtz. Several hundred people died in its cellars. Buried beneath the rubble, their bodies were never recovered.

In July 1945 Austria was divided into four zones, each administered by one of the four powers: France, Britain, the United States and the Soviet Union. The capital city, Vienna, was divided into four corresponding sectors. Although this broadly followed the pattern of the Allied occupation of Germany, there was a novel variation by which it was decided that the centre of Vienna, the Innere Stadt, should be under joint quadripartite control. This arrangement bred the delicious absurdity that helped to give the Occupation its distinctly Viennese character. Each month a different Power would take command of the international force with extravagant military ceremony that must have reminded older inhabitants of the days of the Habsburgs. Whether it was the broad boulevards of the Ringstrasse or the vast courtyards of the Hofburg, Vienna boasted some of the best parade grounds in Europe. It was a city that had been made for marching. Now it was the turn of the victorious powers to preen themselves in the place of the Wehrmacht. Pre-eminent of course were the Americans and Russians, who strove to outdo each other in the splendour of their marching tunes, as soon afterwards they would with their rockets and bombs.

The most obvious projections of power were the hotels that had been commandeered on the Ringstrasse. Gaitered, white-helmeted MPs stood outside the Hotel Bristol, occupied by the Americans. Grim guards with fur hats and bayonets guarded the Hotel Imperial, Hitler's *pied-à-terre* in the days of the Anschluss, and now home to the Soviets. Above their five-star fortresses the Hammer and Sickle and the Stars and Stripes flew in defiant opposition.

While the twentieth century's imperial arrivistes took over the garish palaces on the Ringstrasse, the British took up residence in the Sacher, an elegant building in a quiet little road tucked snugly behind the Opera. An easy walk from the Hofburg, it had been a favourite haunt of the Austrian court. Here Crown Prince Rudolph had given his last dinner party before committing suicide at Mayerling. The Sacher had pedigree. Probably more famous today for its torte, it was here that *The Third Man* was brewed. As a guest in this military hotel, Greene would have been able to witness the workings of the Military Occupation at first hand, and in the film his alter ego, Holly Martins, stays in the same place.

Meanwhile the Viennese looked on with weary resignation, uncertain of what might happen next but extending a practised hospitality. 'Since 1938 we've had to cook for Germans, Russians and now the Americans,' the manager of the Hotel Bristol explained when the March of Time visited in 1952, 'and we always try to do our best to please all our guests.'[7]

Only foreigners could really afford to enjoy the city, which had a curiously deserted air. Madeleine Henrey went there with her film star son in the autumn of 1949, soon after *The Third Man* had opened in London. 'Cafés and restaurants were empty,' she wrote, 'their magnificence and gilded warmth contrasting amazingly with their emptiness, so that one always felt one must have come at the wrong time, but both the will to laugh and the means to do so were lacking.'[8] The kiosks along the Kärtnerstrasse boasted endless entertainments – in Vienna's badly bombed theatres the show went on – but sitting among the audience of barely half-filled houses was 'curiously unsatisfying, as if they were ghosts of something which had thrived in different circumstances'.[9] The round-abouts and shooting galleries had returned to the amusement park in the Prater, but it too, observed Henrey, 'was desolate and sad, as empty, even on a Saturday, as the restaurants and cafés in the city. I have seldom seen anything so strange as the booths all lit up, the steam organs all playing, the showmen all blaring out their lungs for nobody.'[10]

The Viennese concentrated on just getting by. The theatres

and restaurants may have been empty, but the Dorotheum, the government-run pawnbroking and auctioneering house, was doing thriving business. And the Ressel Park – where today's tourists visit the Musikverein or the Karlskirke – had become the centre of a barter economy. Here you might see a Russian conscript selling his food rations; or another with ten wristwatches strapped to his forearm. The *haute bourgeoisie* used to come too, hoping to trade their furniture for food. A bizarre kind of wealth redistribution took place, as the peasants of Lower Austria decorated their cottages with Persian carpets or pictures, and the dwellers of the large Innere Stadt apartments filled their once opulent salons with sacks of potatoes and wheat.

All these transactions shaded into the black market, which was everywhere since money was next to worthless. Gordon Brook-Shepherd, who served as a General Staff officer on the Allied Commission, remembered that he used to pay his driver with packets of cigarettes. To Graham Greene, looking on, the black market must have seemed one of the most obvious things to write about. In the film Anna sells the foodstuffs her British and American audience give her instead of flowers. When Martins tells Baron Kurtz that the police think that Harry is in some kind of a racket, Kurtz replies, 'Everyone in Vienna is. We all sell cigarettes and that kind of thing.'

Another inescapable reality of 1948 was the start of the Cold War. The key months in its gestation coincided almost exactly with the production period of *The Third Man*. In February there was a Communist coup in Czechoslovakia. In April the American Congress approved the Marshall Plan. In June the Soviets began the blockade of Berlin. The Airlift immediately followed, and continued for over a year, ending in September 1949, the month of *The Third Man*'s opening.

Once the Soviets had ceased to cooperate in Berlin, the Allied Commission in Vienna became the only meeting place between East and West. Conflict may have seemed increasingly likely, but in Vienna you could still enjoy the spectacle of a

Soviet officer inspecting the turnout on parade of American
GIs. Its peculiar nature as the last conduit between the two
sides made it a magnet for refugees, smugglers and, not least,
spies. By 1950 more than twenty intelligence organisations
were estimated to be operating there.[11]

As they watched Eastern Europe disappear behind the Iron
Curtain, Vienna's citizens, stranded deep within the Soviet
sector of Lower Austria, must have felt extremely vulnerable.
The Soviets had not won any friends with the brutal manner in
which they had 'liberated' the city. Rape and pillage had been
widespread. Three years on, their occupation still inspired fear,
and there must have been a real sense of foreboding that this
occupation might become permanent.

There was a vast gulf between Vienna's sophisticated if
impoverished inhabitants and the primitive troops who mostly
made up the Soviet occupation forces. The Viennese had
frequent occasion to be staggered by their ignorance. 'When
they were billeted in apartments or houses with proper
sanitation they'd never seen an ordinary lavatory,' Gordon
Brook-Shepherd recalled.[12] 'They saw this inviting pool of
water, and thought that was the place you washed in, and did
their other stuff anywhere else they could find, in a bidet or
even in a washbasin.' Several years later, as a correspondent for
the *Daily Telegraph*, Brook-Shepherd witnessed the departure
of the last Russian troops from Austrian territory. 'It was really
quite pathetic because there were these soldiers, including
officers, many with their families, lugging on to the train
everything they could carry in the way of pots and pans. They
looked like the real refugees.'

So even if there was no open hostility, the strains which
existed between the Viennese and their unwelcome guests
from the East were considerable. But their very lack of
sophistication gave the Soviets an exaggerated respect for both
'Kultur' and the written word. If you were an aristocrat with a
castle in the Russian zone, the best way to protect it from
looting was to write 'Museum' on a placard and attach it to the
front door. British military officials found that the Soviet

authorities always interpreted and observed any rules or agreements literally. In *The Third Man* Major Calloway is minded to overlook the matter of Anna's forged passport, but his Soviet counterpart Colonel Brodsky insists that it be dealt with. This was just one example of the fidelity with which *The Third Man* – even in the tiniest details – captured the contemporary experience of the city.

Vienna was full of Harry Limes in 1948. At first they worked for themselves, but as confrontation between East and West intensified, they found powerful new patrons. In the film Harry's girlfriend Anna is a Czech refugee, whom he betrays to the Russians in return for sanctuary in the Soviet sector. In 1948 there were 600,000 'displaced persons' in Austria, nearly 10 per cent of the country's population.[13] Most of them were from behind the Iron Curtain. The Russians, with the help of people like Harry, did what they could to send them back.

But you didn't even have to be in Vienna to be familiar with these details. Practically every week in the late 1940s British newspapers published stories of kidnappings that the Soviets carried out through their proxies. The victims included refugees, opponents of communism and Austrian officials with information that might be useful to the Russians.

A favourite haunt for the kidnappers and racketeers alike were the sewers that *The Third Man* would make famous. They were effectively an international no-man's-land. You could descend in one sector and emerge miles away in another. The attractions to Harry were obvious, even if finally it would be in the sewers that he met his end.

Greene mixed fact and fiction expertly, but occasionally he must have wondered which had the upper hand. In April 1950, just six months after *The Third Man* opened in London, the newspapers reported the case of gang leader Benno Blum. After the war Blum had operated on the black market in Vienna under various aliases. Then, according to an American intelligence report, he began to kidnap named refugees for the Russians in return for the right to smuggle Hungarian cigarettes into Austria. His gang's activities were exposed, and he fled to the Russian sector for protection. But when the American authorities learnt that he was visiting a girlfriend in the French sector of the city, they organised an ambush – just as the British military police do in *The Third Man*. They stormed the girlfriend's flat. Blum fired at them but his shots went wide. The police fired back, killing him.[14]

3

'Then Along Came This Silly American!'

Graham Greene delivered the treatment – in effect the short novel – to Sir Alexander Korda in late April 1948. Korda decided to go ahead and set off for the United States. The circumstances of the time favoured an American production deal. In March 1948 the British government had announced the Anglo-American film agreement, which limited the amount of British box-office revenue that American film companies could convert into dollars and remit home. One way around the restriction was for Hollywood to produce – or co-produce – films in Britain. Korda had raised this possibility with David Selznick in early April. As both men had a reputation for producing high-quality prestige pictures, it was an obvious partnership. In early May they went on a yachting holiday together in Bermuda. Korda had brought with him one of his chief bargaining counters – Carol Reed. In an agreement which would be signed in New York on 14 May Korda and Selznick agreed to make four films together – of which the first would be *The Third Man*.

The arrangement was that Korda's British-Lion would make the films and Selznick would provide Hollywood stars and a proportion of the finance in return for the American rights. This finance would come from the box-office receipts of Selznick releases in Britain which could not be remitted back to the United States. Just as currency restrictions caused Korda to finance production on the Continent, Selznick (along with a lot of other American producers) was doing the same thing in Britain. British-Lion would also distribute Selznick's American films in Europe. The new partnership began – as it would eventually founder – in an atmosphere of mutual suspicion.

The person chiefly responsible for dealing with Korda was Selznick's representative in London, Jenia Reissar. Only a week after the agreement had been signed, she warned her boss of rumours that Korda lacked the finance for production, and at the same time observed that he wasn't 'telling the truth about some of his connections'.[1] Korda, for his part, would have reason to feel aggrieved when a few weeks later Selznick backed out of the four-picture deal in favour of proceeding on a film by film basis.

During their stay in Bermuda, Reed and Selznick discussed Greene's story in detail. Reed then collaborated with Greene on writing a script, going to Vienna with him for a week in late June for the sake of 'local colour'.[2] A first draft of the script was ready in early July, and the following month Greene and Reed went to see David Selznick in California to discuss it.

In reminiscences Selznick is recalled as something of a caricature mogul, crunching Benzedrine in marathon meetings and firing off ideas that were next to useless. Guy Hamilton remembered that Reed, when he had returned from America, reported back on these meetings with some amusement. 'Selznick marched up and down dictating notes. "Scene one. I think that Harry Lime should be wearing green socks." And he would be marching up and down, and secretaries every two hours would be relieved to carry on taking notes. Well, after about four hours Carol and Greene were looking at each other, and they said, "Would it be possible to have a drink?" . . . And Graham was the first one to get pissed, and went sound asleep. And so Carol kept the ball rolling while Selznick marched up and down, and then when Carol felt like nodding off he woke Graham up. And Graham said, "Would you please repeat that, David, I haven't quite got the essence." And they were forty-eight hours in there, these two.'[3]

Greene himself painted a similar picture. In the Introduction to *The Pleasure Dome*, the volume containing his collected film criticism, he recalled the meetings as long, wearisome and pointless. 'The forty pages of notes remained unopened on Reed's files, and since the film proved a success, I suspect Selznick forgot that the criticisms had ever been made.'[4] Selznick was unhappy with the film's title, Greene recalled, and suggested his own as an alternative. 'What we want is something like *Night in Vienna*, a title which will bring them in.' And on another occasion, Selznick raised something in the script that he didn't understand, puzzling Reed and Greene who could remember no such incident. 'Christ, boys,' eventually he admitted, 'I'm thinking of a different script.'[5]

But as we have already discovered, Greene was a far from reliable commentator, as keen to make the most of a comic opportunity as he was to record the event with any accuracy. He loved a good story too much to let the truth interfere, with his novelist's instinct and his taste for intrigue delighting in the shadow versions of the truth he could weave.

Selznick, indefatigable on his Benzedrine, would certainly have no shortage of absurd ideas, but the evidence suggests that he also made an enormously important contribution at the pre-production stage of the film. Among Carol Reed's papers, at the British Film Institute, there is a two-page summary of the Bermuda meeting. Just about all Selznick's reported comments make excellent sense. The film's famous ending, for example:

> [Selznick] felt that it was a great pity that at the end of the story Rollo [the original name for Holly Martins] and the girl Anna should finish together; we should go from the cemetery scene to Anna going away by herself.
> Selznick felt this very strongly, that Anna's love for Harry Lime should be fatal, especially since it seems impossible for her to be with Rollo immediately after the shooting of her lover.[6]

Greene would later comment that it was Reed who suggested this ending. In his preface to the published story he wrote: 'One of the very few major disputes between Carol Reed and myself concerned the ending, and he has been proved triumphantly right. I held the view that an entertainment of this kind was too light an affair to carry the weight of an unhappy ending. Reed on his side felt that my ending – indeterminate, though it was, with no words spoken – would strike the audience, who had just seen Harry die, as unpleasantly cynical.'[7]

The opinion that Greene attributes to Reed was exactly Selznick's argument in Bermuda, but it's quite possible that Greene was being entirely honest for once. He wasn't present at the Bermuda meeting, and probably wasn't given a copy of the notes. So when Reed suggested the different ending, Greene just assumed that it had been Reed's idea. It was only human nature if Reed, in his discussions with Greene, didn't go out of his way to give Selznick due credit. It was much more fun to lampoon him.

In trying to discover the truth about *The Third Man* an important lesson is that the truth was just about the last thing to concern the most celebrated – and therefore most interviewed – contributors to the film. Greene, Reed, and Orson Welles too, each, in his own fashion, manipulated the truth to his own convenience. Selznick was a victim of this. In the months to come he may often have been as much a nuisance as a constructive force, but none the less his role was far more significant than his English partners were willing to admit – partners who in later years seemed almost to be operating in concert to deny his contribution. 'We didn't accept any of his ideas,' claimed Greene in an interview. 'The trouble was that in the terms of his contract with Korda he was to supply Alida Valli and Joseph Cotten and he had the right of discussion within six weeks before shooting.'[8] In fact, the contract gave him the right not just of discussion but of script approval.

Reed's dismissal of Selznick was, if anything, an even more blatant contradiction of the truth. Speaking in 1971, he would recall him as arguing for the very opposite of what he had done in reality: 'David Selznick had some money in the film (I think it took care of Cotten and Orson Welles' valet). I must say he was very nice and appreciative about the picture as soon as he saw it, but he said, "Jeezez, couldn't we make a shot where the girl gets together with the fella?" "It was in the original script," I said. "We chucked it out." "I'm not sure. It was a good idea." But I mean, the whole point with the Valli character in that film is that she'd experienced a fatal love – and then along comes this silly American!'[9]

Reed's own summary of the Bermuda meeting leaves one much more impressed by how much he and Selznick agreed upon. The character of Anna was clearly a major concern at the Bermuda meeting. She was a significant presence in Greene's original story, but had yet to be converted into the currency of stardom. 'It wasn't a beautiful face,' he wrote of Anna in his original story. 'Just an honest face; dark hair and eyes which in that light looked brown; a wide forehead, a large mouth which didn't try to charm. No danger anywhere, it seemed, to Rollo Martins, of that sudden reckless moment when the scent of hair or a hand against the side alters a life.'

Selznick knew that this wouldn't do, that on the big screen the 'sudden reckless moment' had to be ever-present, that the girl had to be heart-stoppingly beautiful. These were the rules of Hollywood glamour. But where Selznick differed from his Hollywood brethren was the degree to which he empathised with the leading female role. In the past, notably as the producer of *Gone With the Wind*, he had done as much as anyone to establish the strong female roles that characterised so much of Hollywood cinema in the 1940s.

So it was scarcely surprising if he should have wanted Anna, in *The Third Man*, to move more into the foreground of the story. As far as this was concerned, he and Carol Reed were on the same wavelength. Selznick would have admired Reed's 1947 film *Odd Man Out* hugely, in which the strongest character is not James Mason's wounded gunman on the run, but the girl – played by Kathleen Ryan – who seeks to keep him from the police and finally sacrifices herself for her love of him. Indeed here was a prototype for the absolute loyalty that

Anna – at Selznick's prompting – would come to represent in
The Third Man.

Reed's summary of Selznick's remarks suggests that they
were both perfectly in accord on this point. 'It is most
important for the part of the girl Anna to be built up a great
deal more, but since so much of the situation and story
happens around this character, I see no problem here. Selznick
was very keen on Valli playing the part of Anna.'

When Reed and Greene returned from Vienna at the end of
June, Korda cabled Selznick with the news that the 'semi-final
script' the two had written together was a 'tremendous
improvement' on the original story and gave Valli a terrific
part.[10] Selznick received this first draft script a week later, with
a note from Carol Reed. 'Please be as critical as you can,' he
asked, 'as we both know there is a great deal yet to be done,
and that your advice will be invaluable.'[11] It's quite possible
that at this stage Carol Reed was being entirely sincere, but he
could not have anticipated just how critical Selznick would
turn out to be.

Selznick gave a copy of the script to his story editor, Barbara
Keon, asking her in particular to comment on the develop-
ment of Anna as a character. Her response was scarcely
encouraging:[12]

> I think this is pretty bad. Assuming the story is
> interesting enough to be told at all (?), an entire
> rewrite is called for in my opinion. Presently *nobody*
> is treated to any depth of characterisation. We
> understand or care about *no one*. The writing is bald
> and superficial; and frequently there is a bit of
> business or dialogue that is an absolutely meaningless
> tangent, not even valuable for mysterioso. (I never did
> figure out who the 'third man' was.)

Keon was equally dismissive of Anna, the character Selznick
regarded as the 'whole essence' of the Bermuda discussion and
agreements:

> The role of *ANNA SCHMIDT* is certainly not good
> enough for Valli. She never carries the ball, she has
> no dimensions, no transitions, no conflicts ... She
> appears in less than one fourth of the footage, and
> some of that as mere bystander-companion to the
> hero as he trails down clues.

Keon's difficulties with the script perhaps partly reflected a gulf
between European and American attitudes to the movie
heroine. In the heyday of the woman's picture, when the big
female stars were actresses like Barbara Stanwyck, Joan
Crawford and Bette Davis, it was rarely enough in a
Hollywood picture just to be pretty.

Selznick disagreed with her comments. 'You had better be
careful that you're not leading with your chin,' he warned her.
'I was very enthusiastic about the first draft treatment and
think it will make an outstanding picture. Carol Reed is in my
opinion one of the finest picture makers in the world, and is
responsible for this script.'[13]

None the less the reservations of someone he trusted would
have caused him to take extra care to get the script 'right'
when in August Reed and Greene came over for the
conferences. Certainly as far as Anna was concerned, Selznick's
suggestions were aimed at somehow bringing her alive. It
bothered him that she was just a theatre actress. Nothing
glamorous about that. Perhaps instead she could work in a
gymkhana or circus or nightclub – 'something more pictorial
and colorful than the theatre'. While he discussed the issue
into the small hours with Reed and Greene, Barbara Keon
headed a backroom team researching the plausibility of his
suggestions. This time she was careful not to leave her chin
exposed. The team considered every angle.

The circus and gymkhana were out because 'practically the
only entertainment in Vienna now beside the theatre is in the
bars and nightclubs,' reported Keon's assistant Ann Harris.
But, Harris suggested, 'Anna might be an "Animierdame" – a
kind of "B-girl" – those girls who are hired by the nightclub

owners to entertain the guests and encourage them to drink... They get 10% of all the drinks. In better class nightclubs and bars they are not supposed to approach the guests, but to wait until they are invited by the guest to join him.'[14] The deliberations of Keon's team amounted to an expert report on nightlife in post-war Vienna.

Other ways in which Anna might make a living were as a torch singer, piano player in a small bar, hat-check girl, or a female gigolo. Almost every second-class nightclub in Vienna had one or two girls like this. They were paid to dance with unescorted male customers. 'Such a girl does not sit with the customer at the table; she sits alone at a little side-table usually, and is treated more or less like a lady.'

The Vienna nightclubs were listed in the order of their tawdriness. At the top of the list, as the least tawdry, was the Kaiser Bar, which offered dancing, a jazz band and B-girls; at the bottom, the Schiefe Laterne, where a Bohemian crowd gathered to watch a variety show performed on a small stage. Perhaps Anna could be part of this. Reed's standard response was 'We'll think about it', but he and Greene clearly thought that this was just one more ridiculous idea. So a theatre actress Anna would remain. Selznick's general ideas often made sense, but he tended to get hopelessly bogged down in unimportant detail. Much of what Reed and Greene had to endure in the conference amounted to a comedy of useless effort, Selznick with all his assistants playing a kind of Hollywood version of the Grand Old Duke of York.

It also bothered Selznick that Holly and Anna seemed to spend most of their time mooning around her flat or the theatre. He felt that they should be off somewhere having a romantic time. He suggested skiing, and the backroom girls duly conducted some exhaustive research on the logistics. 'The best and most popular ski places are in the Russian zone, and a permit is necessary before an American civilian or a Viennese girl can go there. The nearest and most desirable is the Wienerwald, the hills surrounding Vienna and Vienna's suburbs. The Cobenzl, reached by streetcar (45 minutes), is a steep hill, topped by a small Palais, which has been converted into a fashionable hotel, restaurant and nightclub.'[15]

Anna and Holly swishing down the slopes and then enjoying a little bit of après-ski dancing cheek to cheek in the Palais – it was an example of how a great producer could be capable of the most terrible lapses. His showman's desire for box-office spectacle often undermined the critical discernment of which he was more than capable.

Casting would considerably change the nature of *The Third Man,* and it is in the Bermuda notes that we can trace the steps by which the English characters of Greene's story became American:

> It was suggested that Harry Lime might be played by Orson Welles or Noël Coward, and the part of Rollo by either Cary Grant or James Stewart, but in the event of Cary Grant playing it, it was considered that the balance would be better with Noël Coward, but if it was James Stewart we all felt that Orson Welles would be better casting.
>
> Selznick felt, but was not too definite, about the fact that if Rollo is played by an American therefore Harry Lime should also because what reason would they have for being such close friends. Personally I see no problem here – their families might have known each other, they might have been at school or college together – anyway I don't think anybody would bother about this – we establish that they have been great friends and that's that. The whole story should be going at such a pace that nobody stops to figure that one out.[16]

Of course, in the end Harry Lime was played by an American, and, even if Reed was neutral about such casting at this early stage, he would later become convinced that Welles had to be Lime.

The idea of Cary Grant appearing in *The Third Man* was the

residue of a previous agreement. In 1947 Korda had contracted to make a programme of films for 20th Century-Fox, one of which was described as a 'photoplay as yet untitled, starring Cary Grant'; the contract also stipulated that this film should be directed by Carol Reed. The 20th Century-Fox agreement would fall apart, but Korda still had an understanding with Grant that he would appear in a Carol Reed film.[17]

Grant read Greene's original story and agreed to star on condition that he could play either of the two male leads, making up his mind once there was a finished script. Grant's services would have been expensive – $200,000 plus 10 per cent of the European gross of the picture – but both Korda and Selznick were willing to pay, since they appreciated his huge box-office appeal. Indeed the terms on which Korda and Selznick agreed to co-produce *The Third Man* were several times renegotiated to reflect its changing box-office potential as different stars were considered or became available. At first, Selznick was going to contribute £300,000 to the production costs of the film on the understanding that the very expensive Cary Grant would star. This figure dropped to £200,000 when finally Selznick provided the less popular Joseph Cotten – one of his own contract stars – for free.

Grant eventually dropped out of the project for the prosaic reason that no one could wait for him to make his mind up. Shooting was scheduled for the autumn and there was very little time. 'Grant is out of *Third Man*,' Selznick cabled Jenia Reissar on 16 June. '[I] told him of importance of Reed knowing who was going to play role and after discussion and questions he decided he did not like role of hero and had fears about role of Lime, which however he preferred but would not make up his mind as to either role without script.'[18]

One of the most notable features of *The Third Man* was the number of major production decisions that had to be taken without the existence of a finished script. In this respect it was very much a film made on the hoof. Indeed, Valli only finally got to read her part a few days before she set off from Hollywood to appear in the film.

Reed himself had most wanted James Stewart to play the hero, but would have been happy with Grant. The star he most definitely didn't want – at first – was Cotten. He turned him down when Selznick first raised the possibility in Bermuda. 'I do wish you would reconsider this,' Selznick asked when he later cabled Reed to tell him that Stewart was unavailable, and he urged him to see Cotten's recent films.[19]

The very nature of casting lent itself to a kind of fantasy football approach, which the hyperactive Selznick found irresistible. Even after firm commitments had apparently been made, he was always ready to think again until the last possible moment. It only took a chance conversation or a headline in a trade journal to make him change his mind. So although from his very first discussions with Reed and Korda in May 1948 he had talked of the film as a star vehicle for Alida Valli, he could still raise with Korda in late June the possibility of Robert Taylor and Barbara Stanwyck appearing as Cotten's co-stars. 'They would make wonderful casting in *The Third Man*. My thought of course is that Taylor would play Lime ... the combination of Cotten, Stanwyck and Taylor would be tremendous.' He added thoughtfully: 'But I could not obligate myself to this unless and until I could have the opportunity to find something else for Valli that would make her just as happy.'[20] As at this stage he wouldn't let her see the script, perhaps this wouldn't have been too difficult.

A passing enthusiasm for David Niven even persuaded him out of his initial conviction that Lime had to be American. 'He is superb for perennial schoolboy aspects of Lime's character.'[21] He also noted that Niven was due to appear in a film – *The Elusive Pimpernel* – which would be shot at Shepperton Studios at the same time as *The Third Man*. So it would be easy for the actor to kill two birds with one stone.

Orson Welles had quickly become the firm favourite of Korda and Reed to play Lime. At first Selznick was agreeable to the idea, just as long as Cotten played Martins. 'While Welles has no name value,' he observed in early June, 'he would give it a certain prestige value.'[22] But by September he had changed his mind. One of his contract stars, Robert Mitchum, was doing record-breaking business at the box office. He suggested to Korda that he would be 'superb casting' for Lime and as a star of the first rank would help to build the box office appeal of the film. Welles, by contrast, was according to Gallup a 'detriment'.[23]

Korda cabled 'yes' straight away, but had second thoughts after a long talk with Reed. He sent Selznick another cable: '[Carol] thinks that Orson could give a tremendous performance in this part. Picture greatly depends on Lime being extraordinary in attraction and superior in intellect . . . While I do not profess knowing as much as Mr Gallup about box office values cannot believe him being a detriment. Please give thought to Carol's firm conviction which I fully share.'[24]

Selznick relented and gave his approval to Welles at the end of September, but reconsidered two weeks later after reports that Welles' *Macbeth* looked like being 'one of the greatest disasters of all time in show business'. This, he felt, would make him 'far more of a damaging name than he has been in our worst fears to date'.[25] As Mitchum was no longer available, he fell to recommending Englishmen again – this time Rex Harrison. But Korda told him that it was too late. Welles had been signed. It wasn't quite as straightforward as this, but the presentation of such a *fait accompli* was perhaps the only sensible way of dealing with a man of such maddening volte-faces.

The exchange of telegrams captured a major difference between the two producers. Selznick generally behaved as if no one else's opinion could be more important than his own – or at least the one he happened to be holding at any particular moment. A director's job was to implement his producer's concept of what the picture should be. Korda, by contrast, was prepared to defer to a director in whom he believed. He worked to help Reed deliver his – *Reed's* – vision. The eventual success of *The Third Man* owed much to his unwavering support.

The other leading part was that of the military policeman,

Major Calloway. Korda, Reed and Selznick all wanted Ralph Richardson. He had recently starred in William Wyler's *The Heiress* and so had some name value in America. But Richardson refused the part, believing it to be inferior to the Martins and Lime roles. Reed considered Roger Livesey in his place, but Selznick objected to him as 'difficult for American audiences to understand'.[26]

Trevor Howard was a last-minute choice, signed just before Reed left to begin the location photography in Vienna. You can't help wonder what *The Third Man* would have been like if Richardson had said yes. Howard's Calloway emanates a humanity constrained and shielded by an unflinching professionalism. Richardson's would have been more vulnerable, always seeming likely to compromise himself and transgress the rules out of pity. He was perfect as Baines in *The Fallen Idol* and would have made an excellent Major Scobie,* but his vanity on this occasion was probably a stroke of fortune. You only need to run through a few of the other 'might have beens' of casting to appreciate the importance of chance. If James Stewart had been Martins, it's hard to imagine that Anna would ever have walked past him, just as it seems even more unlikely that she would ever have developed a 'fatal love' for a Harry Lime played by Noël Coward. By contrast, if the Barbara Stanwyck of *Double Indemnity* had played Anna, she would have more plausibly slept with Major Calloway, murdered Harry Lime and run off with the proceeds of the drugs racket.

Reed had not wanted Cotten, Selznick had not wanted Welles, but this unplanned casting added a level, sparking off a marvellous reaction in that indefinable chemistry of filmmaking that depends so much on movie myth and symbolism for its effectiveness. As we watch Joseph Cotten discovering with dismay the corruption of his old friend Orson Welles, somewhere in our cinema unconscious there's Jed Leland, the newspaperman of *Citizen Kane*, coming to terms with the

---

* But when *The Heart of the Matter* was filmed in 1953, it was Trevor Howard who, now having distinguished himself once as a Major in Greeneland, got the part.

bitter realisation that his friend Charles Foster Kane has betrayed his youthful principles.

There was something incongruous in Greene's original story about the English writer penning Westerns. Much more natural that he should be the American he became. And Harry Lime, with his can-do spirit ('He could fix anything,' comments Martins), works extremely well as an example – if a dark one – of American enterprise and individualism. Reed and Greene turned these unforeseen changes to their advantage, adjusting their own conceptions of what the film was about. It took on a new quality, not there in the original story, as a satire of America.

It would be in the handling of Americans that Selznick was most at odds with his English partners. The two leading stars of *The Third Man* may have been American, but they scarcely represent their country at its finest. Welles plays a villain, and Cotten a fool. The true heroes of the piece are the English Major Calloway and Sergeant Paine, who must somehow maintain decency and order, and find their efforts hampered by meddling Americans, well intentioned or otherwise. 'Leave death to the professionals,' Major Calloway tells Martins, as he tries to persuade him to 'go home like a sensible chap'.

Although his efforts would be to no avail, Selznick strongly resisted such characterisation from the outset. The last paragraph of Reed's notes on the Bermuda meeting reads: 'We have to watch very carefully that the balance between the Americans and the British is not weighted in the British or the American favour as far as who are the good characters and who are the bad; but this is no problem, we merely have to remember it.'

One senses here a certain disingenuousness. We get a much better idea of how Reed really felt about Americans from a note among his papers dated 21 May 1948: 'Don't let's forget in the original short story, somewhere at the beginning, a sign saying "American Information Office", which should look very pompous, with the American flag – some suitable music should be playing over it, and as the camera pans down to the entrance officials are going in and out, with a few tarts standing at a respectable distance.'

As far as this aspect of *The Third Man* was concerned, in their conferences with Selznick in August 1948 Greene and Reed were really playing him along every bit as much as Harry Lime would his old friend Holly Martins. They listened patiently to Selznick's demands that America and Americans should receive a positive depiction, and promised they'd do their best, although privately knowing that it did not suit their purpose to do anything at all.

The irony is that probably *The Third Man* wouldn't have been nearly such a satire of the 'American Way' if Greene and Reed hadn't had to deal with Selznick. Just working with him would inevitably have set off a lot of ideas about interfering Americans.

Reading through the pages and pages of conference notes, faithfully set down by Selznick's rota of secretaries, one can find something rather touching about his earnest endeavour, his efforts to help his English collaborators to get the script right. But really he had already had his best ideas in Bermuda. He might have possessed a visceral sense of what worked when it came to the casting of stars and the ingredients of an international movie, but his detailed interventions were rarely helpful.

In Carol Reed's copy of Selznick's conference notes there's one scrawl of 'Very good' next to the suggestion that the beginning of the film should be in documentary treatment, but otherwise Selznick's comments are more notable for their general silliness.[27]

There's no mention in the notes of the title *A Night in Vienna*, which sounds suspiciously like a piece of Greene embroidery, but Selznick certainly wasn't satisfied with the title they had. He suggested that they should think of a new one 'such as "The Claiming of the Body", "The Changing of the Chair" ' or 'perhaps something to tie up with characterisation of Martins'.

Selznick also went to great lengths to patch up what he perceived to be holes in the story. Harry Lime turning up outside Anna's apartment building, his face suddenly lit up in a doorway, may have provided one of the greatest entrances in movie history, but Selznick wanted to know what he was doing there. He suggested that some explanatory dialogue should later be added in the Great Wheel scene:

> MARTINS: What were you doing outside Anna's house?
> LIME: Well, I've always had a secret spot in my heart for Anna. I miss her.
> MARTINS: That doesn't go down with me, Harry. You were going to turn her over to the Russians, weren't you?
> LIME: Yes, as a matter of fact I was.

In this prosaic exchange, which would of course be left out of the final film, there lay a fault-line between two cultures – a European feel for paradox and mystery versus an American urge to explain. In this Cinema of Answers, there must be no scope for ambiguity, the heroes must be heroes, and the villains clearly villains.

Recalling the conferences years later, Graham Greene would write: 'There were times when there seemed to be a kind of grim reason in Mr Selznick's criticisms – surely here perhaps there *was* a fault in "continuity", I hadn't properly "established" this or that. I would forget momentarily the lesson which I had learned as a film critic – that to "establish" something is almost invariably wrong and that "continuity" is often the enemy of life.'[28]

We should not be surprised that in his suggestions Selznick, as he would later put it himself, 'frankly made the Russians the heavies, in pursuit of the girl'. In the finished film, there's no suggestion that the Russians have any nefarious plan – they're just not being very cooperative. In the version Selznick argued for, Anna is kidnapped by the Russians, and we learn that her father was an active anti-Communist, who was killed by the Russians while Anna escaped to Vienna. Not very subtle stuff, but it reflected the attitude of a country in which 'the Reds' had taken the place of the Nazis as the number one enemy. The Berlin Airlift was in full swing, as were the McCarthy witch-hunts in Washington. In the circumstances it was a considerable achievement of Reed to keep the Russians human.

The conferences with Selznick took place over a period of two weeks, from 8 to 19 August 1948. Selznick was so busy that he could only meet Reed and Greene in the evenings. As he kept them up into the small hours, he seems to have taken a kind of macho pride in his display of endurance, which would scarcely have endeared him to his un-sporty guests. 'Do not kill them with overwork,' Korda had warned when he cabled that the two were on their way to America.[29] And more like a football coach than someone engaged in a supposedly artistic endeavour Selznick cabled back: 'I cannot promise Reed and Graham will not return as wrecks since I do not know whether they can take it.'[30] Perhaps if Selznick had got some more sleep, he might have made a better impression on his visitors.

Each session began with a summary of the latest thinking on Martins' character. 'Make him a Southerner (American), with Southern drawl,' read the notes for 8 August 1948. 'Laconic, impulsive, impractical. Went to school in England (schoolmate of Lime's) because his father had some sort of prosaic job in Europe, such as with the American Express or travelling salesman or etc.' A week later the thinking on how Martins came to be in Europe had developed even further: 'An American who had an English mother, who went to school with Lime in England and knocked around in Europe up to the beginning of the war. Perhaps enlisted in English army before breakout of war. Remained in England after war's end.' Selznick, previously concerned that if Martins was American then Lime, for the sake of plausibility, had to be too, had, it seems, by this stage put aside his concerns.

The characterisation of Martins continued:

> Rather unsuccessful in other fields, Martins has turned
> to writing cheap Western thrillers for a livelihood.
> Has never been in the West, and gained all his
> knowledge from movies.
>   He doesn't make much money. Arrives in Vienna
> with a picayune amount of dollars, having spent most
> of his cash in travelling to Lime's rescue and having
> dropped the rest on women en route . . . Rollo is a
> sucker for women and is always being taken. Some
> comedy possible when people always assume Rollo is
> loaded with money because he is an American.

A note followed on the 'Martins–Lime Relationship':

> Need more than schoolboy worship. Lime younger
> than Martins. Martins has always been getting him
> out of jams – from the time when he saved Lime's
> life (where? when?), he has felt responsible for him as
> for a younger brother. Carry relationship through
> recent years . . . were in the war together? Without
> further questioning, when Martins got card or note
> from Lime saying he was in trouble, he has rushed to
> the rescue, merely sending word ahead that he was on
> his way.

All of this was a major reworking of the rather pitiful figure
who featured in Greene's original story. That Martins had
looked up to Lime as if he, Martins, were the younger brother,
and not the other way round. 'He was a year older and knew
the ropes,' he says of Harry in the story. 'He put me wise to a
lot of things.' Likewise, so far from his rushing to Lime's
rescue, it was more Lime who had come to his, inviting him to
come to Vienna, expenses paid, to write about the International Refugee Office, with which Lime was involved. Martins,
broke and badly in need of a holiday, had accepted.
    In the conferences Selznick sought to transform Greene's

no-hoper in to an image of unsophisticated but big-hearted pluckiness. It was a view of themselves that Americans could accept with pride and were familiar with from the movies – Gary Cooper in *Mr Deeds Goes to Town,* or James Stewart in *Mr Smith Goes to Washington* and *Destry Rides Again*; the simple man reasserting civilised values. It was a formula that really went all the way back to Mark Twain (who half a century previously had spent over a year in Vienna himself): in Selznick's mind Martins must have seemed a kind of 'Connecticut Yankee in King Arthur's Court', only now it was Vienna and not Camelot.

Selznick doesn't seem to have hesitated before urging such a major departure from Greene's original characterisation. But perhaps, it just seemed to him a self-evidently necessary change, simply a matter of translation from one medium to another, the difference between books and the movies. Just as the girl had to be beautiful, the hero had to be a hero.

It's difficult to imagine that anyone – apart from Holly Martins, that is – could ever have thought that Harry Lime was innocent. But if Martins was to have any credibility as a hero, it required the audience to see things from his point of view. So Selznick, with his faith in heroes, had a very different conception of the scene in which Major Calloway tells Martins that Lime 'was about the worst racketeer who ever made a dirty living in this city'.

'Audience should be convinced at this point, and for some time in the story, that Calloway is wrong,' record the conference notes, 'and that the police have made a genuine mistake, and that Martins is going to succeed in clearing Lime's reputation. Audience sympathy and rooting interest with Martins. Calloway's offensive personal remarks about Lime should arouse audience resentment.'

But of course in the original story, as in the final film, they don't. The audience knows that Major Calloway is right, and that poor Holly Martins, way out of his depth, is mixed up in something he does not understand. Like the European idea of the typical American – indeed like Selznick himself – he thinks he has all the answers, that it's as clear-cut as the Westerns he writes. But it isn't.

It bothered Selznick that the only authority figures in Vienna should seem to be the British or the Russians. In the conferences he did what he could to redress the balance. He suggested that the film should open with an American general addressing the other representative international powers, telling them of the dreadful conditions in the city due to rackets, crime and profiteering. 'Something has to be done,' the general would say. 'Not merely the people of Vienna are involved but our own nationals as well. Remember the other day, the case of Harry Lime...'

And Selznick suggested the addition of a new scene after Major Calloway arrests Anna for questioning:

> *American Headquarters*
> Martins goes to American headquarters. The
> authorities have heard from Calloway of his conduct
> the previous night and have also got information
> from the Embassy of some affair with a girl in Paris
> on his way through. They warn him that the Lime
> case is a British one and that they have no intention
> of quarrelling with their British colleagues, and that
> he ought to be getting out of Vienna as soon as
> possible, as he's only interfering with everybody.

It was a completely unnecessary addition, its only purpose to show that the Americans were around too, and there but for their grace went the British.

And under the heading 'Background Atmosphere' there was this note: 'Get balance of French and Americans in Vienna, as well as Russians and British. Get Americans in nightclubs, streets, etc., with a couple of good comedy cracks once in a while. As Martins is being chased on street, perhaps he is given a lift by American patrol?'

Although they were perhaps sorely tempted to laugh, Carol Reed and Graham Greene – or whichever of the two was awake at the time – kept a straight face, and listened without demur, believing that when the time came they would do as they pleased anyway.

It is easy to poke fun at Selznick, as of course both Reed and Greene did, but part of the absurdity lay in the nature of Anglo-American co-production. The chief creative personalities may have been British, but the most important market was American. Selznick, who was responsible for exploiting that market, naturally wanted a film that would appeal to an American sensibility.

During their time in Hollywood Greene and Reed met the censors. In a letter of 19 August Joseph Breen, administrator of the Production Code, confirmed that the basic story was acceptable and summarised the agreements that had been reached in conference the previous day:

> There will be no dialogue definitely pointing up an illicit sex relationship between Anna and Harry.
>
> The sequence in the bedroom will be played without any emphasis on the bed, or other sex suggestive flavor to the scene.
>
> In the scene where Anna is arrested and has to dress she will at no time be shown in anything less than a slip, and there will be no suggestive reactions from the soldiers present.
>
> With regard to the ending of the story, Martins' shooting of Harry will be on a direct shouted order from Calloway, and there will be no flavor of either mercy killing or deliberate murder.
>
> With regard to our discussion concerning the drinking and drunkenness present in the script, we again urge upon you the advisability of keeping this down to the very minimum required by characterisation and plot ...
>
> With regard to the killing of the policeman, Paine, please bear in mind the Code clause which states: 'There must be no scenes, at any time, showing law enforcing officers dying at the hands of criminals.'[31]

Rather as he dealt with Selznick, Reed would embrace the censors' comments when they offered an improvement, but quietly ignore them when they were undermining.

Harry's death in the film would completely defy the censors' requirements. Wounded and cornered in the sewers, he gives his old school friend a piteous and pleading look. With a nod, he gestures to be put out of his misery. After a cut-away to where Major Calloway is waiting at the end of a sewer passageway, there's the sound of a shot. Holly then emerges at the end of the passage. The mercy killing had to remain a mercy killing to be true to Greene's original intention. The moment in which a friend kills a friend contained so much of what the film is about. Reed gambled that either the censors wouldn't notice, or that, having complied with so much else, he would be allowed to get away with this particular lapse.

Reed was also determined that Martins should remain a drunk. And in the film he's drinking pretty much at every opportunity. We even see him warming a bottle of spirits in the freezing cemetery as the police dig up Harry's coffin.

Breen wrote again in October 1948 after he had read the final draft of the script, and added a couple of new concerns.[32] In the cemetery scenes it was important that Harry should be buried properly, and he advised the filmmakers 'to get proper technical advice with regard to the religious angles involved'. He also drew attention to the lecture scene, in which a young Austrian, described in the script as having 'rather an effeminate manner', asks Holly Martins where among the great English poets would he place Oscar Wilde. Such a question was 'unacceptable for reason of its obvious inference', observed Breen. 'It will be necessary either to change the question or to change the character of the questioner, to get away from any possible flavor of sex perversion.' It was easy enough for Reed to cooperate. In the film the young Austrian simply asks where Martins would 'put' James Joyce instead.

Selznick thought that the August conferences had gone swimmingly. In their midst he reported to Jenia Reissar, 'getting along well with Reed and Greene despite very considerable changes in script. Present plan is to complete detailed revised outline on which we will be in agreement and script of which will be done by Reed and Greene en route home'.[33] The most pressing problem seemed to be to find an American writer who could turn the Holly Martins and Harry Lime characters into bona fide Americans. It was particularly an issue because, as he explained to Reissar, he had 'sold' Reed and Greene on the idea of characterising Cotten as a Virginian. He thought this would help to supply some much-needed humour. It would also be easy for Cotten to play since he happened to be a Virginian himself: he 'would only need speak like members of his own family'.[34]

It was characteristic of Selznick that he should declare Carol Reed to be one of the finest directors in the world, yet not trust him to sort out the comparatively minor matter of finding a suitable writer. To the irritation of his British partners he sought to involve himself in every detail of the production no matter how small and no matter that he was not actually making the film. He was constantly complaining of overwork, yet throwing huge effort into unnecessary tasks.

As Selznick's chief busybody in London, Jenia Reissar was entrusted with the task of tracking a writer down. He told her to look in Europe, especially Paris and the Riviera, which he regarded as particular haunts for good American writers. He also put forward several suggestions of his own, from Robert Sherwood to Norman Mailer.

But meanwhile Korda and Reed had quietly found a writer of their own, the New York playwright and screenwriter Jerome Chodorov. 'I must tell you nobody ever mentioned it until you,' Chodorov told me when I rang him.[35] Occasionally he had told friends that he had helped to write *The Third Man*, but nobody would believe him, so eventually he gave up.

In the summer of 1948 Chodorov was holidaying in Paris with his wife. He got a call from Korda, who had somehow managed to track him down through his lawyer. Korda asked him if he could rewrite the Holly Martins part, and he agreed to come over to London for three weeks to make Martins an American.

There were very good reasons for choosing Chodorov. He had been in the US airforce during the war, and had worked on documentaries in London with the man Carol Reed would often cite as his favourite director, William Wyler. Through Wyler, Chodorov had met Carol Reed, who was then a captain in the Army Kinematographic Service. So the two men already knew each other and got on. Reed much preferred this to having a Great American Writer imposed on him by Selznick.

'It was the greatest assignment I ever had, sybaritically speaking,' commented Chodorov. 'Things were on the rough in London,' he recalled. 'There was no food to speak of, except at Alex Korda's private den at the Claridge.'

If you were lucky enough to work for Korda, somehow the privations of a country still in the grip of rationing ceased to apply. The American had a Rolls Royce and a chauffeur laid on for him and a suite at the Savoy overlooking the Thames. The deal was a fabulously generous $15,000 for the three weeks' work. But he couldn't get a work permit and officially couldn't be paid. However, Korda, who effortlessly circumvented such obstacles, saw to it that he was compensated with generous expenses and a system of extravagant barter. Chodorov remembers opting for books and silver and foolishly turning down some sound investment advice. 'Zoltan said, "Listen, Jerry, I know a Franz Hals that's available, and it's a museum piece. There'll never be another one like it, and if you buy it you'll be a millionaire some day." Well, he was absolutely right. But I said, "Zoltan, I don't know anything about Franz Hals. I don't know anything about art. I just want to have fun." What a fool I was. Can you imagine? An original Franz Hals.'

His London assignment proved to be a fantastic change from the 'amused contempt' he had been used to receiving from Hollywood producers. 'Writers were zero, the last resort. Few directors believed in writers . . . You know their attitude was: "We could do it ourselves if we had the time, so we hire you guys to do it for us." Really. With some exceptions that was the attitude towards writers.' But now he was made to feel like a valued member of the team.

'Working for Alex Korda was like working for no one else in the world. He was a sultan, a pasha. He was something. Nobody ever treated a writer like he treated a writer ... He knew about writers. And he knew that without the writing there wasn't going to be any picture.'

Chodorov worked together with Carol Reed on the script at Korda's offices in Piccadilly. 'Carol was a very strange duck, there's no question about that.' He remembered that Reed 'would go off into long silences, and look past you into the infinite'. It was impossible to work out what he was thinking. There was also a vagueness there; he seemed not to be entirely in the real world.

One script session was interrupted by a visit from David Lean and Ronald Neame, who also had offices in 196 Piccadilly. They were very upset about the American reaction to their new film, *Oliver Twist*. 'They came in and they spoke to Carol about the fact that the Americans weren't going to release the picture because of Alec Guinness's Jewish portrayal ... He couldn't understand it. He said, "Why are they ... The Jews are doing very well in Hollywood." They said, "That's not the reason, Carol!" He could not understand why the Jews in America were sensitive. This was three years after Hitler.'

But as far as the film was concerned, Chodorov felt that Reed was 'the whole moving force of the thing'. It turned out to be a simple matter to turn Holly Martins into an American. 'I did the job in two days, but I had a three-week deal, so Carol said to me, "As long as you're here, Jerry, let's work on it in three weeks." So I said, "Sure." ' He recalled in particular working on the Alida Valli character, and making the love story strand of the film more plausible. While all this tweaking was going on he met Graham Greene only once. 'We just said hello and he looked at me suspiciously. Nobody likes another writer to come in on his stuff.'

It was understood from the beginning that Chodorov wouldn't get any credit.* It didn't bother him, as at the time he didn't rate the project very highly. 'When I left, I said to Carol, "I wouldn't make this picture, if I were you, Carol." That shows you how smart I was. But I didn't know that the zither player was going to be in it, and that made a hell of a difference that zither player . . . And of course Orson gave it a flavour that it's impossible for anybody else to give. He radiated evil . . .'

A revised version of the script was ready by 20 September. Reed then gave a copy to Joseph Cotten, who was intended to be the chief beneficiary of Chodorov's work. He wasn't very grateful. Jenia Reissar quoted his comments for Selznick: 'We shall have some difficulty over script, but have good story which needs sympathetic treatment, but not by Chodorov.'[36] It confirmed Selznick's general view in life that everything went wrong unless he sorted it out himself. An inevitable barrage of cables followed in which Selznick insisted that he be shown the latest version of the script, that Chodorov be fired and that Reed return to America for a second script conference.

Korda, who had for months bent over backwards to be conciliatory and accommodating, lost his patience. He cabled Selznick on 7 October: 'If you keep on worrying about this script you will cause yourself and myself very distressing time without benefit to mutual interest and quality of picture. You cannot produce a picture seven thousand miles away and you must realize that Carol is not a director of such small stature that in every blessed thing he has to follow ideas put to him on the spur of the moment. For last two weeks Carol has been in constant touch with Cotten, and I have just talked to Cotten on the telephone, who tells me he is in complete agreement

---

* As we have seen, Peter Smollett and Mabbie Poole would share Chodorov's anonymity. The only contributor to the script who enjoyed sufficient fame to challenge this hierarchy of credits was Orson Welles. He was the one person Greene knew he could not deny in his own reminiscences about the film: 'The screenplay was entirely mine,' he would claim, 'except for the passage about the cuckoo clocks, which was written by Orson Welles.'

with script and while he has some objections to some of the dialogue these objections are of entirely minor nature.'[37]

Korda then dismissed Selznick's idea that Cotten should play a Virginian as 'an artificial idea in no way helping film'. It might have seemed a very small matter, but this upset Selznick most of all. It was like Desdemona's handkerchief, throwing into doubt the trust he had given. In an angry memorandum he insisted that Jenia Reissar should take issue: 'To say that the idea of the Virginian is artificial is ridiculous, and I would like you to so characterize it to Reed and Korda. How can I accept the sincerity of their statements when they tell me that it is "artificial" for a Virginian to play a Virginian? Why is it more "artificial" for the character to be a Virginian than for him to be a New Yorker or a Texan?'[38] He went on to question whether he had been kidded along at the conferences: 'If I was to take at face value the things that Greene and Reed agreed to, I should expect a different attitude, and one indeed of appreciation; if on the other hand, I was deceiving myself as to their reactions, and have been deceiving myself since as to what they intended to effectuate with the rewrite, then I certainly have been led up the garden path and the picture cannot go forward, because the contract specifically provides that the final screenplay shall be in accordance with the notes.'

Selznick was of course right to be suspicious, just as Reed and Greene were too good a director and a writer not to want to make the film their own way, even if this meant deceiving him. It was a classic vicious circle. People didn't confide in Selznick because they feared his interference. And he interfered because people didn't confide in him.

At about the same time as Jenia Reissar was dealing with her boss's concerns about the script, she raised her own about costumes. Carol Reed had rung up to tell her what he wanted Valli to wear in the film. He asked that she should bring with her from Hollywood one or two of her own suits, a skirt, sweaters and blouses. He wanted her to wear them in so that they didn't look new, as Anna wouldn't have been able to

afford new clothes. He also said that he would prefer it if she
didn't wear a dress because the sort of dress Anna would be
able to buy would look awful, and a well-cut one would look
too chic. Reissar summarised her conversation with Reed in a
letter to Selznick, commenting: 'Personally I can't see why
Anna shouldn't have good clothes, as presumably Lime would
have given her some. It seems a pity to have Valli wear such
intensely uninteresting garments!'[39]

Selznick cabled back, 'Feel it incredible that as sophisticated
a black marketeer as Lime would not have supplied his girl
with attractive and exciting clothes including lingerie and wish
you would discuss this with Alex, Carol and Greene.'[40]

Reissar sent a copy of Selznick's cable to Korda, with this
note: 'I am not writing to Carol, as I feel Mr Selznick's
comments should go to you, and I should appreciate it very
much if you would let me know whether you agree with Mr
Selznick. I think Valli would be so much happier if she could
wear nice clothes, and really there is every reason to believe
Lime would have bought these for her. Surely her shortage of
money would date from Lime's disappearance – but that
would not affect her clothes.'

It's difficult to know quite what Reissar was expecting to
achieve. Quite apart from the obvious disrespect she was
showing Reed by going behind his back, Korda would have
scorned such petty powerplay. His reply revealed him once
again as eager to back Reed's judgement as Selznick was to
overrule it:

> Carol Reed feels very strongly and I fully agree with
> him that to put a glamorized Valli in the Viennese
> atmosphere will kill the whole realism of story. We
> do not feel that silks and frills make a woman more
> attractive than simple clothes especially if the
> atmosphere demands nothing else. We are convinced
> that Valli in a macintosh and beret can be as
> attractive and charming as many stars wearing fashion
> creations. Also it would be harmful to Anna's
> character to suggest that Lime set her up in an

apartment or that she has accepted expensive gifts from him even if he could obtain them in Vienna today. Carol's aim is to make Valli as glamorous and attractive as possible without sacrificing absolutely essential truthfulness of story.[41]

A few days later Carol Reed himself explained to Reissar why Anna could not be dressed more smartly. Reissar duly listed them for Selznick in a contrite letter:

(a) The audience does not know that Lime is a black marketeer until the last reel. Suspense would be destroyed if his activities were disclosed at the beginning.

(b) Lime never tells Anna that he is making money, as she would obviously guess at his illicit dealings if he were to provide her with a lot of fine clothes, and by so doing, Lime would also draw attention to himself, since it would arouse suspicion that the girl he is known to be associated with – a small part actress very poorly paid – is dressed in expensive clothes.

(c) Even the people who have money in Vienna today do not wear elaborate clothes, because it is so out of tune with the surroundings and the dire poverty of the Vienna population. Those who have money, legally or otherwise, *do not* make themselves conspicuous.

(d) Lime proves to be an absolute rotter and the audience must feel intensely sorry for Anna whose love for him was genuine, whereas she really never meant anything to him. The fact that he betrays her for his own advantage, shows the type of man he is.[42]

In the film the most luxurious thing we ever see Anna wear is a pair of silk pyjamas with the initials HL on the breast pocket. It conveyed both Anna's love and Harry's vanity. The only nice things he ever got were for himself. It was a wonderful touch which perhaps Reed would never have thought of had not the whole issue of costumes been put into his mind. Many times in the course of the making of *The Third Man* such apparently unhelpful interventions would prove to be the grit in the oyster.

None the less, the constant scrutiny and interference were taking their toll on Reed, as he sought to make clear to a now remorseful Jenia Reissar. He felt disheartened and disillusioned, he confided. Never had he felt so harassed over a script. 'Carol said that he would sooner get right out of the whole thing than have endless trouble . . . He said he felt now that he would rather make a picture with English artists and be left to his own devices, than have American stars and lose his interest in the film.'[43]

Chastened, Reissar backed off. But Selznick suspected plots everywhere. Korda had promised to send him a copy of the final script straight away, but why had he taken so long to do so? Why had Reed dismissed the Virginian idea, although he had agreed to it in the conferences? What guarantee did he have that Reed wasn't going back on other things that had been agreed? He drew up lists of Korda's contract violations, no matter how minor – although he certainly couldn't claim innocence himself in such matters. Most ominous was a breach of the requirement to deliver a 'final screenplay' sixty days before the first day of principal photography. Its arrival just as Reed was about to depart for Vienna only increased Selznick's misgivings.

Back in London Reissar had checked it against the previous draft and the conference notes with her assistant. 'In our opinion almost every point and suggestion has been incorporated either directly or by implication,' she reported.[44] By contrast Selznick recognised an excellent script, but was still furious because in his opinion it departed from the conference notes over the most essential issue – the treatment of the Americans.

In a cable to his 'Foreign Co-ordinator', Betty Goldsmith, in New York, he declared: 'I am convinced that Reed has no

Burying Harry Lime in the late autumn of 1948. Alida Valli stands by the Familie Elchinger tomb.

The same spot in the autumn of 1998. Harry would have borrowed Johann Grün's grave, just across the way from the Elchinger's. Since Harry's burial, time has added a few more names to the Elchinger and Grün memorials.

The statue of Josef II, where, according to Baron Kurtz, Harry was laid down to die after being run over by a truck. The lights are set up to film the entrance to Harry's apartment building, while the Viennese, in the Josefsplatz, look on. Carol Reed stands in the foreground in a pair of big boots and a duffle coat.

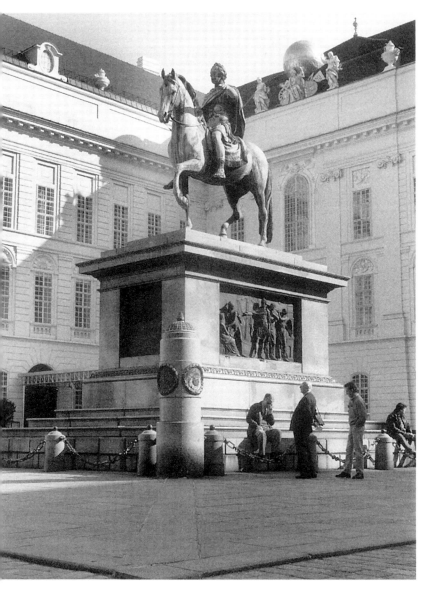

The Josefsplatz today, the National Library behind restored to its pristine grandeur.

Off-duty publicity: Joseph Cotten delivers America's Marshall Aid to the children of Vienna.

Back to work: Holly Martins (Joseph Cotten) questions the Porter (Paul Hoerbiger) in the entrance to Harry's apartment building. Note the continuity 'goof' of the street number. When Holly arrives in Vienna, he tells customs officials that he is going to stay with a friend of his at 15 Stiftgasse.

Little seems to have changed at No. 5 Josefsplatz in fifty years. Impervious to time, Harry's girls look as beautiful as ever. And even the same net curtain hangs in the left-hand window – although curiously the Italian words of 1948, QUADRI ANTICHE, are now in French: TABLEAUX ANCIENS.

1945: 'Bombed about a bit…': The Am Hof, where Harry Lime disappears down into the sewers.

The Prater. The Great Wheel, minus its carriages, miraculously survived a battle between the Red Army and the retreating SS.

Entrance to the sewers, by the Stadtpark U-bahn. The sewers are built around the Wienfluss. The River and Sewer authorities share responsibility for looking after the tunnels, much as the Four Powers once carved up the city above.

Below: Harry Lime first appears in the doorway of No. 8 Schreyvogelstrasse (on the right), his face caught in light from the upper windows of Schubert's one-time favourite haunt, the 'Drei Maderl'. Before Holly can catch him, he runs around the corner…

…and into this lane half a mile away. Sadly restored now, fifty years ago it boasted a marvellous crumbling wall and glistening, uneven cobbles that demanded dramatic licence.

familiarity whatsoever with our rights in the matter; and therefore has seen fit to take only those changes which suit him and Greene from the standpoints of English storytellers, making the picture for English audiences.'[45] He went on to outline his specific objections:

> The script is written as though England were the sole
> occupying power of Vienna, with some Russians
> vaguely in the distance; with an occasional Frenchman
> wandering around; and with, most important from
> the standpoint of this criticism, the only American
> being an occasional soldier who apparently is merely
> part of the British occupying force, plus the heavy
> (Lime), plus the hero ... and just to make matters
> worse, the American hero apparently is completely
> subject to the orders and instructions of the British
> authorities, and behaves as though there were no
> American whatsoever among the occupying powers,
> nor any American authority, and indeed as far as this
> picture is concerned, there is none. It would be little
> short of disgraceful on our part as Americans if we
> tolerated this nonsensical handling of the four-power
> occupation of Vienna ... I went through this at the
> greatest length and in the greatest detail with Reed
> and with Greene, and come hell or high water, I
> simply will not stand for it in its present form.

It's in such angry outbursts of indignation that Selznick comes most to resemble Holly Martins, the American in Vienna mistrustful of the British authorities with which he has to deal. He even had an inkling of the parallel himself. 'The British are doing enough to us without making us stooges and, to use the term of the script, "bloody decoyed ducks", for spreading their propaganda. I have had enough of their finagling and their machinations.' Somewhere in his subconscious mind probably Korda had become Major Calloway.

He was so suspicious of British intentions that he began to question the ultimate loyalty of the English Jenia Reissar, even though she had worked for him for over ten years. She had given such a positive report on the script, and in recent days had distinctly mellowed in her attitude towards Korda and Reed. 'Without in any way challenging or impuning her unquestioned and highly valued loyalty to us, we must remember that she has superior loyalties as an English subject,' observed Selznick in his cable to Betty Goldsmith.

With his fears of betrayal and hidden conspiracies, Selznick would have slipped comfortably into a Graham Greene novel. But he was not the sort to allow a potential mole in his organisation to go any length of time unchallenged, and quickly called upon Reissar to explain herself. In a memo dated 19 October she replied:

> You will, I am sure, agree it is difficult to judge a revised script on short notes written for the purpose of reminding those present at the conference of points discussed in detail. While I know these notes are perfectly understandable to you, Carol, Graham Greene and Miss Keon, some of them seemed to me to be contradictory and I just had to use what I thought was common-sense in evaluating them...
> I did not realize, and frankly I don't see how I could from the notes without having heard your arguments on these points, that the American angle was of such importance to the American market since we have Cotten and Valli – both well-known in the American market – to carry the picture.
> ... some of the notes on the four-power situation seemed to me a matter of background, atmosphere and documentary shots. After my conversation with Carol, when he pointed out that the story was basically one showing Vienna today, I felt convinced that he would take care of those requirements in the notes since he is spending over two weeks on the background shots before he gets any of the principal artists over...[46]

She couldn't resist a final barbed paragraph, which if it didn't quite amount to 'leading with her chin', was certainly sailing close to the wind: 'I think you are right in saying in your cable that an English woman's point of view is probably very different. I rather think we see things from a more realistic angle, but then our newspaper stories are more factual and subdued than the occasional American papers I see.'

With Carol Reed already in Vienna and principal photography scheduled to begin in a few days' time, Selznick now resorted to a strategic weapon for imposing his will. Alida Valli, who was supposed to arrive in Vienna on 1 November, was still in Hollywood. He instructed her that she should take the train, and not fly, to New York, and then take the boat to Europe. 'But we will not permit Valli to sail from New York until and unless there is expression from Korda and from Reed on what we regard as absolute necessary additional scenes and rewrite to meet requirements in accordance with contract and with notes of conferences.'[47] As Valli trundled slowly across the wilderness of America – at last with a script to read – she would have had plenty of opportunity to ponder how Anna Schmidt must have felt to be a hostage to fortune.

Selznick's ultimatum had the desired effect of concentrating minds. It was agreed that he and Korda would meet in New York to settle their differences, but, Selznick made it clear, 'I will not leave for a meeting with him in New York unless he clearly expresses himself as a basic principle of this meeting that he is going to live up to his contract, and that he is going to force his director-producers to live up to it.'[48] No longer would he fall for Korda's 'blandishments and blarney', he declared.

But that was precisely what he then proceeded to do the following week when the meeting took place. Korda was adept at turning such face-to-face encounters to his advantage, and persuaded Selznick that with one exception all his desired changes should be left to Reed's discretion – after all, he did have the right to demand retakes if he was unhappy. The exception was that Reed should be obliged to depict America's role in Vienna as an occupying power in a way that corresponded to the true facts. But this was a vague requirement, which did not practically restrict his freedom. A written memorandum of agreement was drawn up on 26 October, and Valli was allowed to sail for Europe on the *Mauretania* the following day.

Selznick, who was constitutionally incapable of relaxing, still bombarded Reed with notes for how the script might be improved, but Reed knew now that he could safely ignore them, leaving Korda to defuse the situation. 'Mr Reed is in the middle of a very hard and responsible job, working day and night,' Korda finally wrote to Jenia Reissar's assistant after several weeks of silence (Reissar herself was in hospital). 'Therefore he cannot be expected, and I am sure Mr Selznick does not expect him, to sit down and write copious answers on copious notes.'[49]

For the length of the film's production, at least, the silly American was effectively forgotten.

4

On Location

Production facilities were provided by Sascha Films which had studios in the Viennese suburb of Sievering. Korda had directed several films there just after the First World War. His old friend and colleague Karl Hartl now ran the company. Sascha Films advanced two million schillings (about £50,000) to finance the location expenditure. In return, they were given distribution rights to a number of Korda's old films.[1]

Stars and crew were all booked into the Astoria Hotel on the Kärntnerstrasse. The first day of principal photography was 22 October 1948, and the last 11 December. On 15 December the production then transferred to England, where shooting recommenced on 29 December, finally finishing on 31 March 1949.

On the surface it seemed a crazy schedule. Location pictures were never shot in the autumn and winter unless they were set in tropical jungles or the frozen wastes. Likely rain, sleet and snow, coupled with the shortness of daylight hours, made shooting an impracticality. What made *The Third Man* different was that most of the shooting took place at night. When it rained, it actually helped in a film which depended so heavily for its atmosphere on the glistening cobbles of night-time streets. It simply saved the need to get the fire brigade to wet them down.

It helped too that much of the shooting was to be done in the main sewer of the city. Built around the Wien river, a tributary of the Danube, it was about thirty feet wide, and – with its high, barrel-like ceiling – made a perfect studio, warm and cosy regardless of what the weather might be doing outside. There were a few day exteriors, but so few that it was a reasonable gamble to fit them in during the seven-week shoot.

The biggest danger was snow. In Vienna winter can come early, and Elizabeth Montagu remembered Carol Reed voicing his fears about this. Occasionally snow did fall, and the production would switch to the sewers. But the big race was to avoid the heavy falls which would be bound to arrive at the end of the year.

To make the maximum use of time, shooting was organised into three units, each with its own lighting cameraman. Robert Krasker was in charge of the night unit, Stan Pavey the sewer unit, and Hans Schneeberger the day unit. But Carol Reed directed all three, day and night, around the clock. There was no second unit director, he didn't approve of them. Guy Hamilton, who, as his loyal assistant joined Reed in this punishing schedule, remembers the routine. 'The night unit finished at 4 or 5 o'clock in the morning, and you'd have three hours sleep till 8, because it didn't get light until about 9 o'clock in the morning... You couldn't shoot day after 4 o'clock in the afternoon, so from 4 till 7 we got three more hours' sleep then. And somehow for 7 weeks, 3 hours there and 3 hours there, and lots of Benzedrine, Carol directed the whole sodding thing.'[2]

The only exception was the documentary preface explaining the four-power occupation of Vienna. It was shot by Hans Schneeberger's unit after the British crew had returned home. If you look carefully, in these early shots you can see the snow which had finally arrived and is entirely absent from the film proper.

No scenes were shot at Hartl's studios in Sievering, but it was the provider of lights and generators and props. Bob Dunbar was a production assistant. One of his jobs was to fill a truck full of baroque bric-à-brac – statues and lamp brackets and so on – which was to be on hand during the shooting. Reed would then pick something out and stick it up somewhere to add a little extra to the shot.

*

Carol Reed was perhaps the supreme scissors-and-paste director. What mattered to him was that a scene should *feel* authentic, not that it should necessarily *be* so. Take for example Harry Lime's famous first appearance. In the film it happens like this: Martins sees Harry's face lit up in the doorway. He starts to cross the road between him and the door, but a car suddenly appears out of nowhere, momentarily halting his progress. When at last he gets to the doorway, Harry is gone, and all that can be heard is the sound of his footsteps. Martins runs round the corner in pursuit. He's in time to see the shadow of Harry's running figure, cast huge against a wall, but not Harry himself. Martins runs down the cobbled street, casting his own shadow on the wall, and then through an arch into a huge square, but Harry has vanished.

This sequence – from Harry's appearance in the doorway to Martins' arrival in the square – takes place in about thirty seconds, but brings together several widely dispersed locations. The doorway was at No. 8 Schreyvogelgasse – 'Shriekbird Lane' – a street which, with its picturesque eighteenth-century houses, had often attracted film crews seeking to recreate old Vienna.

Opposite No. 8 was the Dreimäderlhaus, so called because according to legend Schubert had kept three of his girlfriends *(drei Mäderl)* there. But in *The Third Man* there's just one cross middle-aged lady, who looks out to see who's making all the racket. The arrangement of buildings was perfect for the light from the upper-storey windows of the Dreimäderlhaus to seem to fall upon Harry's doorway. But with almost every shot there's a falsification of reality. The beam of light itself was more like a searchlight than anything a sixty-watt bulb could produce. Then there's a cut to Harry's face, which was actually lit up some weeks later in a substitute doorway in Shepperton. If you look closely, for the first split-second the doorway's in darkness although the light has already come on in the previous shot. This delay might not have been true to the speed of light, but the switch out of darkness makes a much more dramatic entrance for Harry.

There's a medium shot of Holly looking on bemused. Mid-distance in the background can be seen a group of statues and in the far distance a gothic church, lit up although it's late at night. Neither the statues nor the church are actually there. It's just a three-second reaction shot, but Reed went to such lengths to fill it with enriching detail.

The light in the window goes off, and just as Martins is about to cross the street the car comes along. Anyone familiar with the Schreyvogelgasse will know what a piece of dramatic licence this is. You'd have to wait hours to get run over there – it's just not a place that cars normally go, especially not in the middle of the night (and especially not in 1948).

The shot of Martins running across the road is on the Schreyvogelgasse, but he runs around the corner not into Molker Steig – the street which is really around the corner – but into Schulhof. This street was a good half mile away, but boasted a wide expanse of wall and some picturesque lancet windows. It was superb for casting dramatic shadows, but also opened into the Am Hof, the largest square in Vienna. Harry possesses a supernatural quality. In a place where there should be nowhere to hide, he still manages to find somewhere.

A judiciously placed water basin, filled with the pee of a stone putto, even made it possible to capture Martins' exasperation as his quarry eludes him. The sequence ends with him splashing his hand in the water with frustration. This fountain must have come off Bob Dunbar's truck. Before I visited Vienna I thought I'd recognise the square by its presence. I found the square but not the fountain. Passers-by thought I was imagining things when in my bad German I asked about *die Fontane* which used to be by the entrance to the Schulhof. I was.

Carol Reed took a particular delight in weaving such disparate images into a believable whole. Guy Hamilton remembered how on his next film, *Outcast of the Islands*, 'he shot a scene seamlessly between Trevor Howard (Sri Lanka), Robert Morley (Shepperton Studios) and a small Malay boy in Indonesia. None of them ever met.'[3]

Reed used to send Hamilton off every night to collect 'faces', which he would then use – a little like Bob Dunbar's bric-à-brac – to add atmosphere. They would be onlookers to witness the drama unfolding in their midst, briefly distracted from their own lives by the commotion, as the fugitive makes his escape or a pursuing car flashes by. 'I used to go down and collect them from the soup kitchen,' Hamilton recalled. 'And he'd say what did I learn? One night I said, "I found someone absolutely marvellous. You'd love him, Carol. He's got no nose, and looks like the Hunchback of Notre Dame." And he said, "Guy, Never make fun of people with disabilities." He really had a go at me. And still today when I see *A Fish Called Wanda*, I can't stand it, because it makes fun of stutterers.'

It is this compassion that helped to make Reed such a great director. He took every bit as much trouble with the residents of the soup kitchen as he did with Alida Valli or Orson Welles. He possessed an ennobling eye, which – however far it may have wandered from a conventional reality – invested a scene with a poetic truth.

His approach was instinctive rather than intellectual. Probably he didn't even articulate clearly to himself why he had done something, he just felt that it 'worked'. But what he chose as a piece of storyteller's craft always possessed a deeper level, capturing something true.

Major Calloway and Sergeant Paine hide outside the café where Martins has arranged to meet Harry Lime. It's a moment of great suspense, as they wait for Lime to show up. Reed felt that some kind of comic relief was required to sustain the dramatic tension. What he devised was this. A huge shadow is thrown up against a building as a figure approaches. It's not Harry Lime but – of all things at this time of night – an old balloon-seller, with his balloons on a pole. He approaches Major Calloway and Sergeant Paine, and offers them a balloon, which is the very last thing they want to think about. Sergeant Paine buys one to get rid of him.

What might, in another director's hands, have been awful became in Reed's a sublime moment of un-scripted cinema, a perfect fusion of comedy and pathos. It was also an excellent example of making the most of a location. The suffering and the endurance of the Viennese can be traced in the balloon-seller's lined features. It made a huge difference that he wasn't an actor, just as it made a huge difference that the Vienna we see on the screen wasn't a studio set. The poor old man really did eek out a living selling balloons in the Prater, and you could just imagine him – in a way it would have been impossible with an actor – somehow finding himself with his pole of unsold balloons in an empty night-time square. The impoverished, divided post-war city, with its desperate inhabitants, threw up such absurdities with ease.

Reed had spotted the old man in the Prater some days before. Probably at that stage he just made a note of a striking face and filed him away in his mind as having potential for something, without his knowing quite what. But now he had found a concrete way in which he might be used. Guy Hamilton remembered how shooting this scene had unfolded:

> [The balloon-seller] comes along, and he's got his
> pole with all his balloons on, and he's a nice old boy,
> and he's half asleep because he's been working all
> day. And Carol says to him that he go round to
> Trevor and say, 'Balloon, balloon, mein Herr, buy a
> balloon.' And the old boy mumbles something in
> German. Carol says, 'What the hell's he talking
> about?' And I say, 'That is the German for balloon.'
> 'But it looks as if he's asking him for money. No, no,
> no.' Right there and then he says, 'You go up and
> you say, Balloon.' 'Carol, that's not the German for –'
> 'I don't give a fuck.' So he then teaches [him] and
> the guy says, 'Balloon.' 'No, no. Bal-loon. Bal-loon.
> Bal-loon.' So this old boy for the first time in his life,
> who doesn't know what he's saying, goes, 'Bal-loon,
> bal-loon'.[4]

Carol Reed has often been compared to Alfred Hitchcock, the cinema's proverbial 'Master' of suspense – and the comic relief that such suspense so often entails. But in Hitchcock films these moments are two-dimensional and narrow in their purpose. In Reed's they open up a world. You can construct an imaginary life for the balloon-seller in a way that would be nonsensical for most of the bit players drifting through Hitchcock's films. That famous Hitchcock quote – 'Cinema is life with the dull bits left out' – was much truer of Carol Reed than it ever was of Hitchcock, whose devotion to artifice was total. He was as much a creature of the studio as Carol Reed was of the location. The stuff of reality was vital to Reed, even if he manipulated it to his own ends. Hitchcock, one feels, could never have made a *Third Man*, because he took so few chances.*

On 31 October Joseph Cotten and his wife, Lenore, arrived in Vienna from Italy. Elizabeth Montagu remembers that at first they were rather upset. The Russians had stopped their train at the Semmering Pass, on the border between British-controlled Styria and Russian Lower Austria; here they had been pulled out of their compartment in their nightclothes, and searched on the line.

Montagu thought they were 'the easiest people in the world'.[5] If there were any nights free of filming, they seemed to prefer to spend civilised evenings at the hotel. Lenore was an excellent pianist, who would occasionally be persuaded to play. But although they appeared to be the picture of a happy couple, they were in fact attempting to patch up a badly shaken marriage. A few months previously in London, where Cotten had been appearing in Hitchcock's *Under Capricorn*, his wife had discovered that he was having an affair and she attempted to commit suicide. To aid her recuperation they spent three weeks before *The Third Man* holidaying in Europe.

Although outwardly contented, Cotten was in a crotchety mood that autumn. In London he had already expressed his

---

* It's worth noting that Hitchcock did have occasion to make a film set in Vienna. *Waltzes from Vienna* (1933) was a failure, in part because he lacked the spontaneity and lightness of touch that such a musical required.

misgivings about the script, and he was no happier to be in Vienna. Soon after his arrival he complained to Jenia Reissar of the 'appalling inefficiency' of the British unit.[6] It probably didn't help that he knew he hadn't been Reed's first choice for the part. Selznick was so worried about his attitude that he suggested that he be made to watch Reed's previous film *The Fallen Idol* in order to cultivate a proper degree of respect (although seeing the film hadn't made Selznick any more respectful). But it wasn't really necessary because in practice Cotten's tendency was to be pleasantly cooperative in front of the cameras while complaining in private. He was an actor after all.

Three weeks into filming he telephoned Selznick to say that he was miserable in Vienna and deeply disturbed that he was going to be stuck there three times longer than the two weeks originally planned. He blamed Carol Reed for being so slow. 'I gather that fault is because Reed is getting only about one shot each day and one shot each night,' explained Selznick in a cable to Jenia Reissar's colleague in the London office, Louis Lewis (Reissar was still in hospital). 'Joe does not want to be in middle of this and clearly should not be placed in position of being critical of Reed since this could affect relationship upon picture most damagingly. He requested we find some reason for inquiring and for doing what we can to expedite things.'[7]

Lewis cabled back that Cotten's schedule was actually four weeks, which he ought to have known, and that although there had been some delay it was largely due to the late arrival in Vienna – as well as frequent departures from Vienna – of Cotten's close friend Orson Welles. Cotten was now due to finish in Vienna on 8 December, which was only three days later than had originally been planned.

Jenia Reissar's assistant, Rosemary Clifford, rang him on 27 November to cheer him up. 'His mood definitely seemed to have improved,' she reported back to Selznick, 'though he is no happier about being in Vienna – nor, I gather, is Mrs Cotten – than he has been all along.'[8]

On December 8 Cotten left with his wife for Paris, where he

was asked to stay for three weeks to avoid having to pay British tax. He'd already spent several months in England making *Under Capricorn*, and the weeks to come filming in Shepperton Studios were likely to exhaust his exemption. He seemed much happier to be in Paris than in Vienna, but none the less complained about the uncooperative attitude of London Films towards promptly paying his expenses while he was there. If the manager of his hotel – the Lancaster – had not recognised him, he told Jenia Reissar incredulously, he would have had to pay the bill himself![9]

Cotten's various complaints offer some insight into the lot that film stars have to endure, and his travails didn't stop when he got back to London. He and his wife were expected to stay in the Savoy. It was inconvenient for the shops, and he thought it would be difficult for his wife to get around, especially in bad weather when taxis seemed to vanish off the streets. He asked if they could be put up instead in Claridges, where at least his wife would be within walking distance of restaurants and hairdressers.

Reissar put in a request with London Films on his behalf. Colonel John Codrington, who was responsible for accommodation arrangements, spoke personally to the manager, to be told that the hotel had been completely booked up because of a government conference.

'The question of accommodation in London is quite appalling,' he replied apologetically, 'and few people realise what we are up against. The Manager of Claridges remarked that Mr and Mrs Cotten were extremely lucky to be in the Savoy!' He suggested that Cotten speak to Sir Alexander Korda, who had a penthouse on top of the hotel. 'As he is living there, he can sometimes pull off something which I am unable to do.'[10]

Back in London, Cotten began to hit the bottle again. Elizabeth Montagu remembered him pouring whisky after whisky. 'He was knocking them back. The bottle was gone. He was drinking too much. They were all hard drinkers.'[11]

It must inevitably be speculation, but perhaps one of the

reasons why he was so miserable in Vienna was the strain that keeping to the straight and narrow could have on a constitution unused to such discipline. Before his wife's attempted suicide he was, as he put it in his memoirs, living the life of Riley. 'I was an actor. A roamer. A lover. I made pictures, I made love, and I made martinis.'[12]

But in Vienna he was the only actor who had taken his wife along. Her presence there was exceptional, because the city was still short of food, and military permits were only being issued to foreigners who had work to do in the city. Alida Valli had to leave behind her four-year-old son and nanny. Mrs Cotten was only allowed in because the occupation of 'secretary' happened to have been written in her passport and she was 'attached' to the unit.[13]

However determined Cotten might have been to patch up their relationship, it must have been hard to stay in the hotel listening to his wife play the piano while his fellow actors went off every night to get plastered.

In the film Holly Martins is the drunk, and Major Calloway stays sober. In real life – at least in Vienna – it was the other way round. Even at this relatively early stage in his career, Trevor Howard had secured an unchallenged place at the top table of the drunken actors' hall of fame. The tales of his drinking exploits make his performance as the cool and professional Major Calloway seem all the more extraordinary – as astonishing a confidence trick as Harry Lime running a medical charity. With Joseph Cotten temporarily on good behaviour, the only person who came close to him was Bernard Lee. They were as much a drinking team in the bars as Major Calloway and Sergeant Paine were an investigative team in the British army.

For Guy Hamilton, as assistant director, an important consideration was to arrange the night shooting so that the two actors could get to their favourite nightclub before closing time. They wouldn't finally turn in until about 6 o'clock in the morning, so it was another challenge to get them up again for the next day's work. 'The trick then was to charge in at 9 o'clock in the morning and to say "COME ON, YOU'RE LATE, YOU'RE LATE, YOU'RE LATE!"'[14]

On one occasion Trevor Howard was in too much of a hurry to get to the bar in time to change out of his Major's costume. After a few drinks, he got into an argument, and the noise attracted a real major.

'Who's that Major there?' he asked, to be told that it was Trevor Howard the film actor. 'Well, he shouldn't be wearing the king's bloody uniform.' He called the MPs, who came around to arrest a spy.

By coincidence the film crew was shooting at Allied Headquarters that evening. Bob Dunbar was there when the call came in. He rushed over to the nightclub to find two Majors standing face to face embroiled in a furious slanging match. One of them was Trevor Howard. An international patrol of policemen – British, French, American and Soviet – looked on giggling to themselves, and a large crowd of the other drinkers in the bar had gathered round. They were all on Howard's side, clapping everything he said, which only made the real Major even more angry.[15]

Dunbar got Howard to make some sort of an apology and sent him home to get changed. But the incident had to be reported and Howard was summoned before the British commanding general – Lieutenant-General Alexander Galloway.

Whatever problems Howard's drinking might have caused, at least one always knew where to find him. A much more serious difficulty was Orson Welles' failure to arrive in Vienna until long after he was due. It was decided as far as possible to double for him. Guy Hamilton was one of the people who acted as his stand-in. He became adept at running in front of an arc light and sending a shadow scurrying down alleyway walls. To hide the fact that he wasn't Orson Welles, he wore a big hat and a black coat, and Reed made him leave a coat hanger in to bulk out his much slimmer frame. Although at

the time everyone was far too busy to notice or care, fifty years
on it seems oddly fitting that Welles should turn out to be
someone else just as Harry Lime in his coffin turns out not to
be Harry Lime at all but Joseph Harben.

In 1948 it was hard to go anywhere in Vienna without running
into the occupation forces of one or other of the four powers.
It contributed enormously to the atmosphere of the film, but
also had its risks, particularly in the Russian sector of the city.
The two chief locations there were the Great Wheel and the
railway station, the Sudbahnhof. Careful permission had to be
sought well in advance, but sometimes even that wasn't
enough. Guy Hamilton remembered being sent off with a
camera to film a bridge. The crew climbed to the top, then got
down to find themselves surrounded at gunpoint by Russian
soldiers, who confiscated the camera.

On another occasion soon afterwards Carol Reed was
filming in the Sudbahnhof itself. After one take, remembered
Hamilton, a Russian officer arrived. The filmmakers had long
ago been given permission to shoot, but after the bridge
incident it was clear that permission didn't really mean very
much. If the Russians – whose occupation of Austria had
generally been characterised by the appropriation of property
on a massive scale – felt like taking the camera they would take
it. 'We're all saying, "Get . . . The . . . Bloody . . . Film . . .
Out . . . of . . . Here. Take one," And the camera crew are
unloading, and the clapper boy is running around in circles.
"But we have permission to shoot." "I did not grant
permission." And Carol says we'll go again. Take two. And
they are actually filmed.'[16]

By contrast – no doubt spurred on by general resentment of
the Russian occupation – Vienna's mayor and city officials
went to huge lengths to help the filmmakers in any way they
could, stopping the traffic, mobilising the police force, sending
out the fire brigade, or doing whatever else they could to be
useful.

On 19 December, a few days after the British crew returned

home, St Stephen's Cathedral opened its doors to the public for the first time since the war. In the last days of the fighting it had been shelled with incendiary bombs by the retreating SS troops. A fire raged over four days and nights, consuming the fifteenth-century timbers of the roof and sending the cathedral's bells crashing through the floor into the catacombs below. Now over three years later, at last it had been restored to its previous Gothic splendour. The snow that the filmmakers had so feared had finally arrived in time for Christmas and the feast of St Stephen – which would have had a special significance for the Viennese that year.

As evening fell, the rebuilt cathedral was lit up by the powerful arc lights that had been used to shoot *The Third Man*.* It was the filmmakers' parting gift to the city.

---

* Mole-Richardson type 1450–225 amp 'brutes', supplied by a Mole-Richardson 1,500-amp silent generator.

5

Stealing the Limelight

During the making of *The Third Man* Orson Welles was every
bit as elusive as his fictional counterpart. From the very
beginning the whole pattern of his involvement in the film was
that of a man on the run. Michael Korda in his book, *Charmed
Lives*, tells an amusing story about accompanying his father,
Vincent Korda, on a mission to bring Welles back to London
to agree terms. They flew to Rome and turned up at the Grand
Hotel, where Welles had last been sighted. Here they
discovered that their quarry had moved on to Florence. When
they arrived in Florence, they were told that Welles had just
left for Venice. The chase continued up and down Italy,
Vincent and Michael always arriving just a little too late, until
finally Welles was cornered in his favourite restaurant, the
Bonne Auberge in Cagnes-sur-Mer. Vincent got him drunk,
bundled him into a private aeroplane and took him back to
London.[1]

Having at last persuaded him to sign a contract, they should
have tied him up and put him in a box to Vienna. Instead,
they just let him walk out of the office. Welles was always
signing bits of paper, but it was quite another matter to get
him to honour them. On the loose again, he went to Rome,
where he was to be found – with the usual difficulty – in
November of 1948. After several days of shooting without him,
Reed decided that someone would have to be sent on another
kidnapping mission.

Bob Dunbar was chosen and briefed carefully. As Guy
Hamilton had been running around as Lime for some days

now, the wardrobe of big black coat and hat was fixed. Dunbar was to explain this to Welles and then take his measurements as if his prompt arrival in Vienna was just a matter of course. If he met with any resistance, he was gently to persuade him of the fabulous opportunity the part represented. 'Carol's scenario which he gave me to persuade Orson was brilliant because Carol used to be an actor himself. My line was to persuade Orson that he had a very small part, and just to imagine anybody sitting in the cinema, and for ten reels [the story's] boring the pants off them, and you come in in the eleventh reel and steal the film.'

Dunbar recalls that they met at the Castello di Sant'Angelo. Welles, who had been acting in the Renaissance epic the *Prince of Foxes* (made, incidentally, for 20th Century-Fox), appeared dressed in full costume as Cesare Borgia. He was in a friendly but contrary mood. 'We got pissed together, it's not difficult with Orson, and I booked him on a train. But then he refused to answer the phone. He'd bribe the telephone operator at the Excelsior Hotel to say he wasn't there. And I started bribing her to put me through.'

Finally Dunbar had to resign himself to returning to Vienna alone. The ever-affable Welles asked him to go back via Venice to pick up some suits for him – just in case he should change his mind. When Dunbar arrived back in Vienna, 'there of course on the platform was Orson and Carol. [Orson] made out this was one of the biggest jokes ever he was playing on me, but I knew damn well that he was leaving it until the last minute.'

But Welles' participation in the film was probably less a stroke of fortune that it seemed to people at the time. *The Third Man* was actually the much-delayed first assignment in a three-picture deal that he and Sir Alexander Korda had signed back in September 1946.[2] For 10 per cent of the producer's gross receipts and an advance of $75,000 dollars Welles would come to Britain to work for London Film Productions 'as either artist and/or director and/or producer' on three films. In the nine-page letter agreement Korda's lawyers set out in minute detail exactly what London Films expected of Welles. Such pettifogging precision could rarely have been more necessary, given Welles' Protean ability to wriggle out of commitments.

Clause nine of the agreement made it clear why Korda was prepared to go to such trouble: 'It is distinctly understood and agreed that the services to be rendered by you hereunder and the rights and privileges herein granted to us by you are of a special, unique, unusual, extraordinary and intellectual character . . .'

The first film Korda wanted Welles to make was Oscar Wilde's *Salomé*. It was scheduled to begin shooting in Technicolor in January 1947, but was put back because Welles was still in America working on *The Lady from Shanghai*. Korda and Welles then argued over who should play the title role and the project was eventually abandoned. Welles prepared several other projects for Korda, including Pirandello's *Henry IV*, *War and Peace* and *Cyrano*, but these all fell through too. 'I lost several years of my life *not* making pictures for Korda,' he would later comment.[3]

As it was proving difficult to find a suitable film for Orson Welles to direct, Korda decided by mid 1947 to employ his services as an actor instead. A provisional slate of London Films productions drawn up in June 1947 included 'a photoplay, as yet untitled, to be directed by Carol Reed, starring Orson Welles, or both Ralph Richardson and Michèle Morgan'.[4] Long before *The Third Man* had been thought of, Korda had anticipated that Carol Reed and Orson Welles could make an attractive partnership.

In the event Carol Reed would make the film with Ralph Richardson and Michèle Morgan – *The Fallen Idol*. But Welles was still under contract to Korda, who had ample leverage with which to secure his appearance in Reed's next production. So when Welles was fetched back by Vincent Korda from Rome, it wasn't to sign a new contract, but to vary the terms of the original 1946 agreement. Instead of $75,000 and 10 per cent of the gross receipts, Welles, who was desperate for cash to finance his filming of *Othello*, settled for a flat $100,000.

'I knew I was going to do it,' Welles would later say of *The Third Man*, 'but I was going to make Alex *pay* for all those movies I hadn't done.' Hence the games he played with Vincent Korda and Bob Dunbar. 'I thought if they really want me for this, they're going to have to chase me, and I'm going to make it just as unpleasant as possible.'[5]

To put Welles' fee into context, Selznick had estimated the dollar cost of Joseph Cotten (had he been hired out on another film rather than given to Korda for free) as $175,000.[6] But given the general feeling in Hollywood that Welles was as likely to turn people away from cinemas as draw them in, his $100,000 was doing extremely well. Korda's association with him at this time would have seemed as much an example of his expensive tastes as his Havana cigars, and he was careful to keep the prior agreement a secret from Selznick. One of the stipulations of their production deal was that Selznick should have copies of all the actors' contracts. But when inquiries were made about Welles' contract, the reply came that none existed. If Selznick did not seem particularly bothered by this technical breach at the time, probably it was because Welles was viewed more as a liability than an asset. If there was no contract, asked Selznick's lawyer, did that mean then that the Selznick Releasing Organisation were free not to use his name at all in the advertising and billing of the American release?[7]

Welles may have been disappointed not to have directed any films under the Korda contract, but he made full use of Korda and London Film Productions as milch cows to support his own *Othello* project. In April 1948 Korda sanctioned the payment by London Film Productions' Italian office of 3,000,000 lire to cover Welles' living expenses in Italy, although Welles had no contractual entitlement to this money.[8] There was also an informal agreement whereby London Film Productions would provide logistical support for the *Othello* production. Welles grossly abused this arrangement, diverting all his various bills, whether for hotels, film stock or cigars, to London Films, with no obvious intention to pay them.

Korda was happy to indulge Welles so long as there was a use for him, but began to tighten the purse strings once Welles had safely completed his role in *The Third Man*. If any one event marked the moment when the two went their separate ways, it was perhaps Welles' armoury expenses, incurred in late 1949. Rather than settle a hire fee for '6 armour breast plates, 6 buck plates, 6 helmets, 6 pairs of grieves, 6 pairs of pauldrons, 6 cross handled swords and 6 daggers', London Films preferred to let Welles be sued for non-payment.[9] The message was clear: Korda had had enough. Soon afterwards he also had the last laugh by assigning the remainder of Welles' contract to Herbert Wilcox, producer of such confections as *Spring in Park Lane* and *Maytime in Mayfair*. If Welles had thought it impossible to abase his art any further after acting in such leaden Hollywood films as *Black Magic* or *The Prince of Foxes*, it was time to think again.

When Welles finally did turn up in Vienna in the middle of November 1948, the crew had been shooting so long that his arrival caused little excitement. Just one more actor. His first scene was in the sewers. Carol Reed noticed some water cascading down from a duct. Wouldn't it be wonderful, he suggested, if the fugitive Harry Lime were to run underneath this fall. The water pouring down on his face offered marvellous scope for drama. One might have expected the greatest ham in the business to be excited by the possibilities, but Welles just exploded. He launched into a tirade, furious that he should be expected to work in such filthy conditions.

The British crew, who had been happily putting up with the filth for several weeks now, were rather taken aback but there was nothing they could do except watch him storm off. 'Well,' said Reed, 'it's his first day, he's nervous, and we've got so many other things to do. We will just have to build a sewer in Shepperton.'

Given his refusal to go down into the sewers there was really very little for Welles to do in Vienna. He 'had one day's shot walking to the Prater wheel, and walking away from the Prater wheel,' recalled Guy Hamilton, 'and I think I'm right in saying that was the sum total of Orson's Viennese contribution.'[10] All the shots of him in the sewers took place many weeks later at Shepperton – with its more hygienic water supply.

At Shepperton Welles was scarcely more accommodating. 'He made life as difficult as possible for everyone,' recalled John Hawkesworth, the assistant art director. He said I'm so busy – which was quite untrue – that I can only give you a week at the studio. So I had to build all the sets which he was involved in all at the same time.'[11]

Some of the recollections of Welles in London suggest a vulnerability at odds with his bravura image. Joseph Cotten, who knew him better than anyone else, thought he was a great director but not a very good actor. Elizabeth Montagu, who became good friends with Cotten, was struck by how nervous Welles seemed during the Great Wheel scene. There was one shot which had to be taken over and over again although he had only a few words to say. 'Every time Orson fluffed it. Orson was sweating, and I said to Joe that evening, "What happened?" He said, "Well, it was the first time that Orson had to act with me and he knew that I didn't think much of the way he did things and he was nervous." '

If Cotten made him feel uncomfortable as an actor, Reed was as formidable a rival in the directing stakes. Bob Dunbar – the unfortunate dupe of Welles' tricks in Rome – thought that, behind all the games, Welles was genuinely afraid of working with Reed. Critics may today celebrate Orson Welles as a giant of the cinema, but at the time it was the British director who was riding a tidal wave of acclaim. On both sides of the Atlantic his film *Odd Man Out* had been declared a 'masterpiece' with an extraordinary unanimity, and he was considered among the best half-dozen directors in the world.

By contrast, Welles, for all the obvious brilliance of *Citizen Kane* and *The Magnificent Ambersons*, was regarded in the industry as dangerously wayward and box-office poison. None of the Hollywood studios wanted to employ him as a director – that's why he had come to Europe – and, as Selznick's own reluctance indicated, they weren't much more interested to have him as an actor. He must have been rather envious of Reed, who was regarded as one of the world's great directors but also enjoyed the kind of commercial success that Welles never had.

This was upsetting enough, but to make matters worse Reed's latest film *The Fallen Idol* had opened in London to ecstatic reviews in the autumn of 1948. It's not fanciful to imagine him ruminating over the cuttings in his room in the Excelsior – perhaps helpfully sent to him by London Films as an assurance that he would be working with the very best of directors. It might have been great preparation for *Othello*, but it would hardly be surprising if it made him hesitate to pack his bags for Vienna. Having accepted that challenge, he was determined not to be eclipsed, and made sure to leave his mark.

In Shepperton he would do some running about on the sewer set and stand in a doorway a few times, but the core of his performance was the dialogue scene with Joseph Cotten at the Great Wheel. The style of the film changes to accommodate his larger ego. Welles is not the kind of actor to stay silent any longer than he has to – he barges in on Cotten's lines in a manner that is reminiscent of the overlapping dialogue in *Citizen Kane*. As nearly all the actors did, he tailored his lines until they felt comfortable, but in substance the scene was played as scripted, until it came for Lime to take his leave of Martins. Then there were hoots of laughter as Welles tried out a few extra lines of his own:

> In Italy for thirty years under the Borgias they had
> warfare, terror, murder, bloodshed – but they
> produced Michelangelo, Leonardo da Vinci and the
> Renaissance. In Switzerland they had brotherly love,
> five hundred years of democracy and peace, and what
> did that produce ... The cuckoo clock?

'Fine,' said Reed, and the cuckoo clock speech was shot.*

Ever since it has been quoted as an example of Orson Welles' brilliance. In fact, it was stolen. 'It was Orson who remembered the gag about the Swiss cuckoo clock and so on,' recalled Bob Dunbar. 'But he didn't invent it, he just remembered it. I remembered it too. And I was supposed to find out where it came from. We were going to shoot in half an hour. How the hell was I going to find out? Go to the British Museum? It would have taken me three weeks.'[12]

Probably the speech derived from a passage in James McNeill Whistler's 'Ten o'Clock' lecture – named after the time of its evening delivery on 20 February 1885.[†] 'False,' declared Whistler, was 'the fabled link between the grandeur of Art and the glories and virtues of the State, for Art feeds not upon nations, and peoples may be wiped from the face of the earth, but Art *is*.' In what seems now a rather ornate and overblown manner he rounded off this theme with an example of Art's fickleness:

> A whimsical goddess, and as capricious, her strong
> sense of joy tolerates no dullness, and, live we never
> so spotlessly, still may she turn her back upon us.
>
> As, from time immemorial, she has done upon the
> Swiss in their mountains.
>
> What more worthy people! Whose every Alpine gap
> yawns with tradition, and is stocked with noble story;
> yet, the perverse and scornful one will none of it, and
> the sons of patriots are left with the clock that turns
> the mill, and the sudden cuckoo, with difficulty
> restrained in its box.

In fairness it has to be observed that Welles' theft was a big improvement upon the original, turning Whistler's rather

---

* In a recent parlour game to prove that Harry Lime was wrong about the Swiss in five minutes we could only come up with Jean-Jacques Rousseau and Max Frisch.
† I'm grateful to a member of the audience at an NFT showing of *The Third Man* who told me about Whistler, thus saving *me* three weeks in the British Museum.

long-winded and pompous preaching into something funny and startling.

The cuckoo clock speech made it clear that Welles wanted to be more than just an actor saying somebody else's lines. But perhaps he would have intervened earlier had he not already been so firmly the focus of attention. 'If Orson had to listen to Joe Cotten playing the scene,' commented Guy Hamilton, 'he would have said, "Carol, how about . . . I get so bored with all of this, how about if I opened the door of the carriage and did that?" If it had been the other way round, that would have been it, but as Orson was totally in charge, they played this scene well, to script.'[13]

Welles was much more difficult to handle when he had no lines to say. Elizabeth Montagu remembers that on the sewer set he argued with Reed about the manner in which Harry Lime was shot. He suggested an alternative way for how it might be done. As their discussion became more heated, Reed – infinitely accommodating, but sly – appeared to relent.

'Now look, Orson, I think what you've just said is very very interesting and really marvellous. I wish to God I had thought of it first. But look, we've set up this shot, it's quite difficult, I think we'd better get on with it, and then when we've shot it, we'll do it your way.'[14]

Happy with this concession, Welles cooperated as the scene was first shot Carol Reed's way. But, recalled Elizabeth Montagu, it seemed to go on for ever, Carol Reed wanting take after take because something or other wasn't quite right. 'I couldn't see what was wrong, and then of course the penny dropped to me. Eventually he stopped, and he said, "Ah, yes, I think we've got it now," and by that time Orson was practically buckling at the knees. That was the testing ground. Carol was very clever.'

Interviewed on the set at Shepperton, Welles commented, 'As a director I soft-soap the actors. I caught Carol Reed doing that with me the other day – and what was worse, I found myself believing him. Carol and I have one thing in common – we are both awfully patient with me.'[15]

*

Welles' own account of his involvement in the film is a mixture of extravagant claims and false modesty. But film critics were so eager to attribute the film's perfections to him that it must have been hard not to play along just a little. This interview with Peter Bogdanovich, for example:

PB: Besides playing Harry Lime, what else did you do on it?

OW: I wrote my part –

PB: Every word of it?

OW: Carol Reed is the kind of director who'll use any ideas – anything that's going. I had notions for the dialogue, and Carol liked them. Except for my rather minor contribution, the story, of course, was by the matchless Graham Greene . . .

PB: Did you have anything to do with the actual set-ups and shots in the picture?

OW: Just a very few *ideas*, like the fingers coming through the grille.

PB: What about the first time we see you in the doorway?

OW: Pure Carol. He had a little second-unit specially set up for it, and at the end of every day we went there and tried it again over and over, till he thought it was right.

PB: Was the last scene at the funeral your touch?

OW: No, it was not. It was a great shot invented by Carol – not by Greene or anybody else. Wonderful idea. I was there when they shot it. I wish I could pretend I'd contributed, but I was just standing there, watching them shoot it.

PB: The picture seemed influenced by you ... perhaps
because of the casting of [Joseph] Cotten.

OW: It was Carol's picture, Peter – and Korda's.[16]

For all his show of modesty, Welles' little nose would have
been a bit longer by the end of this interview. 'I wrote my
part ...' 'I had notions for the dialogue ...' These are extravagant claims which are not borne out by an inspection of the final
draft of the script. Apart from the cuckoo clock speech and some
lines about not being able to get indigestion tablets in Europe
(Welles himself was a sufferer), Harry Lime's dialogue is
otherwise in essence, if not always word for word, as scripted.

But the tendency of film writers to treat him as an all-
accomplishing genius made such theft easy. To read the
various published accounts of Welles' involvement in *The
Third Man* is to trace the making of a movie myth as far
removed from the truth as, say, Greene's portrayal of Selznick
as a caricature film mogul with no useful ideas whatsoever to
contribute.

'The final chase through the sewers,' wrote Peter Cowie in *A
Ribbon of Dreams: The Cinema of Orson Welles*, 'seems to have
been directed by Welles, to judge from the similar sequence in
The Trial when K flees from Titorelli's studio. As in *Journey
into Fear* one cannot help suspecting that Welles may have had
a hand in certain vital scenes.'[17] But since *The Trial* was
actually made in 1962, more than a decade after *The Third
Man*, this is if anything slightly less plausible than to suggest
that Carol Reed was partly responsible for the look of Welles'
The Trial – which no one would dream of doing.

Carol Reed's own casual and often false recollections of *The
Third Man* served only to feed the process of Chinese whispers
to the advantage of Welles' ever-inflating reputation. In 1956
he was quoted in Peter Noble's *The Fabulous Orson Welles*:

Orson suddenly turned up one morning, just as we
had set up our cameras in the famous sewers. He told
me that he felt very ill, had just got over a bout of
influenza and could not possibly play the role. He

apologized profusely, but said that he had
reconsidered his decision and had really decided
against doing the picture.

As I had the cameras and crew all waiting to go I
begged Orson to change his mind. I entreated him, in
any case, just to stay and play the scene we had
prepared, where he is chased along the sewers. I told
him that if, afterwards, he was adamant in not
playing in the picture we could still use the shot, as it
would show only his back.

Reluctantly he agreed. 'Those sewers will give me
pneumonia!' he grumbled, as he descended the iron
steps. We shot the scene. Then Orson asked us to
shoot it again, although I was satisfied with the first
'take'. He had some idea of how to play the scene
more dramatically. He talked with the camera-man,
made some suggestions, and did the chase again.
Then again. The upshot was that Orson did that
scene ten times, became enthusiastic about the story –
and stayed in Vienna to finish the picture. And, of
course, he gave a miraculous performance.[18]

The quotation has the Sunday-supplement tone of someone
who had over the years become practised at telling journalists
what they wanted to hear. Reed was more concerned to
provide entertaining copy and to be nice to past collaborators
– people with whom he might well have to work again – than
to tell the truth or reveal its more unpleasant complexities
(such as Welles storming off and a sewer set having to be built
in Shepperton). If he had any particular purpose it was simply
to explain how he had got Welles to become fully involved in
the picture, thus eliciting the 'miraculous performance'.

The passage became a departure point for subsequent
Welles biographers, often used to support the familiar image
of the errant genius that the world wanted Welles to play.
Take, for example, Charles Higham's biography, *Orson Welles:
Rise and Fall of an American Genius*, published soon after
Welles' death in 1985. It's impossible to be completely certain
because Higham does not provide source notes, but the

following is probably an embellished version of the Reed quotation:

> He turned up on location as Reed was preparing with camera-man Robert Krasker* to film the scene in which Lime is pursued by the police through the sewers. Welles was not dressed for work, and Reed was shocked. Welles said he was feeling ill, having just gotten over influenza, and could not go ahead; he was very sorry, but he could not make the picture after all.
>
> Reed, with his entire crew and cast standing by, urged Orson to change his mind and to play the scene because otherwise it would cost Selznick a fortune, delay the picture, and possibly put people out of work. Welles was impressed with Reed's determined manner and gave in. Yet the smell of the sewers and the intense damp worried him, subject as he was to asthmatic seizures and sinus attacks, and only with reluctance did he change into Harry Lime's clothes and, un-athletic as always, descend awkwardly the narrow iron stairway into the sewer.
>
> He played the sequence with intense discomfort, then, perfect though he had been, insisted it was not good enough. The long-suffering Reed stood back while Welles talked with Robert Krasker, suggesting angles and a use of shadows that greatly enhanced the sequence. It was not Reed's custom to shoot many takes, but Welles wanted at least ten repetitions of every scene; on several occasions he also told Krasker precisely how he wanted to be lit. Captivated by his performance, Reed accepted everything. Once again Welles was influencing the direction of a film he appeared in.[19]

With the appropriate embroidery, Welles becomes the Great

---

* Higham assumes that 'the camera-man' Reed mentions is Robert Krasker. But if this incident had indeed taken place in Vienna, which seems very unlikely, then the camera-man would have been Stan Pavey, who was in charge of the separate sewer unit.

Artist, and the 'long-suffering' Reed, is made in the comparison to seem the dependable but uninspired craftsman, settling for the early take rather than going the extra mile to achieve perfection. One would let such false accounts pass were it not for the tendency of other writers uncritically to repeat them, until soon they receive widespread acceptance as the truth. And now they're being perpetuated in the electronic age. It was irritating, although not surprising, recently to look up the film on the Internet Movie Database and read, under the heading of 'trivia', the following comments: 'Orson Welles wrote all of his own lines in the picture and practically directed the scenes in which he appeared.'

Carol Reed was Welles' equal as a director, albeit of a very different kind. To say so may be to fly in the face of received opinion, but then it is opinion as often as not received from such distorted accounts as Higham's. Reed did whatever was necessary to achieve the effect *he* wanted, occasionally – this much is true – indulging Welles' sense of self-importance: 'There was one take,' recalled Bob Dunbar, 'when Orson kept on saying, "Well, I could do it better," and we went to take 37, and Carol just let him go on. Carol knew he was going to use take 3, which he did, and it got worse and worse.'[20]

6

In the Studio

Back in England shooting began on Wednesday 29 December 1948 in the small London Films studio at Isleworth. The first scene to be filmed was of Major Calloway treating Martins to a drink in a Kärtnerstrasse beer cellar. Then the film crew moved into Harry Lime's flat, where they filmed Martins interrogating the porter about Harry's accident. The Austrian actor Paul Hoerbiger couldn't speak a word of English. His difficulties perhaps inspired those of his character, who several times has to ask Anna how to say things in English.[1]

His helpers in real life were the Viennese director Paul Martin, who explained what the words meant, and then Elizabeth Montagu, who taught him to speak his English lines phonetically.

Meanwhile studio sets were being built at Shepperton. Based on photographs and on-the-spot sketches, these were designed by Vincent Korda with his assistants John Hawkesworth, Ferdinand Bellan and Joseph Bato.[2] Hawkesworth remembered that about 75 sets were built.[3] In preference to the usual rather elaborate, glamorous settings of the studio, the emphasis was on building small realistic sets that matched the original Vienna locations.

On Thursday 6 January work switched to Shepperton, where filming began on a set of the Casanova nightclub based on the real Casanova in Vienna. The following week, as Reed continued to film on this set and also to do some street scenes outside Harry's flat, huge efforts were made to prepare for the arrival of Orson Welles. On Shepperton's Stage B Vincent

Korda supervised the building of the main sewer in Vienna.[4] As Welles was not prepared to spend more than a week in the studio, all the sets for his scenes had to be built at the same time. 'We had a night gang and a day gang,' remembered John Hawkesworth, 'it was hell really, the amount of work.'[5] A separate camera unit under John Wilcox lined up and rehearsed back projection shots for the Great Wheel scene. The idea was that Welles should be able to step in front of the camera without any delay at all.

Welles arrived from Paris on Sunday 16 January and began at Shepperton the next day. With the aid of the two units Reed achieved a near-miracle of finishing Welles' scenes within the week. The first four days were spent with the back projection shots in the carriage of the Great Wheel, and the last two on the sewer set. Even after Welles had gone, Reed continued to use a second unit. It made it possible for him to save time by filming several of the less important shots while the main unit was changing from one set-up to another.

Although what was an important shot? The most famous in the whole film – Harry in the doorway – was shot by John Wilcox's second unit, as Welles himself recalled. It's not that far-fetched to suggest that the second studio unit was Welles' most important contribution to the film. Were it not for his prima donna behaviour, probably there wouldn't have been one, and it would have been far more difficult for Reed to lavish such care and attention on these supposedly minor details.

The second unit stayed in the doorway to film Lime's cat. Reed wanted the creature to come along, look up and then play with Harry's shoelace. 'I cannot tell you what agony this was,' recalled Guy Hamilton, the 'cat director'. Two cats had been used in Vienna, and two more would be used in Shepperton. The first belonged to Hamilton's landlady, but then she went on holiday and took it with her. Another one had to be found. 'And this was a really stupid moggie, and so we put sardine on the shoelaces. It didn't work. And then we had an extra and he had a piece of thread that went down his trousers to the shoelace. He pulled it up and down in the vain hope that the cat might play with it.' The creature made Orson Welles seem a model of patience and consideration. Thousands of feet were shot in the attempt to deliver the performance that Carol Reed wanted. 'At the end of rushes every day on came the moggie shots and the theatre emptied, and I'm saying, "Carol, I think that at about 800 feet there's a bit that you'll like. . . ." '6

Working every day during the lunch hour with the editor Oswald Hafenrichter, Carol Reed would put together an assembly of the footage so far shot. On Wednesday nights everyone would gather to look at the latest rough cut. It was a way of seeing how the film was progressing, and made it possible to correct an actor's performance or to add a missing ingredient to a scene. Sometimes these sessions could decide the whole direction and mood of the film. One night, recalled Guy Hamilton, everybody was captivated by a particularly beautiful sequence:

> There were about ten or twenty of the most beautiful
> shots of Vienna . . . that were magical – the rhythm
> of the cutting, the photography, the everything. And
> we used to sit looking at the rough cut, and say, 'You
> know, you can't do black and white photography
> better than this . . .' Suddenly the lights went up and
> Carol was white and sweating. He said, 'It's got to
> go.'
> I said, 'It's the best bit.'
> 'You don't need it, it's dead footage.'
> I said, 'Carol, maybe story-wise it's dead footage,
> but it's just unbelievable, it's so lovely and beautiful
> and we spent months shooting the sodding stuff.
> Don't make up your mind now.' The following
> Wednesday Carol was wrenching his guts out because
> it was so beautiful, but you can tell the story, and the
> story demands that you go from A to C and you
> don't need B . . . It hurt him, and I'm sure he had
> sleepless nights, but he knew that you had to go from

A to C, and although B was beautiful, fabulous, it
had to go into the cutting bin.

For Reed the story was paramount. He could plumb the
deepest depths of character, squeeze out every last drop of
atmosphere and tension, but always he did so in service of the
story.

A visitor to Shepperton during these weeks would have found
a surreal jumble of different sets scattered across the huge A
and B stages. Some abutted on to each other. The cinema in
which Martins and Anna briefly take refuge, for example,
shared a wall with the children's hospital that treats the victims
of Harry Lime's diluted penicillin. And next to it, by a macabre
coincidence, was a set of the cemetery.
The great tribute to the three Hungarians and Englishman
of the art department is that just about everyone who sees *The
Third Man* assumes that it has been shot entirely in Vienna. In
fact, many shots of the city had to be recreated at Shepperton,
calling for extraordinary feats of matching. Crucial to this
process was the stills photographer Len Lee, who had taken
thousands of photographs of every detail of contemporary
Vienna. In the case of the cemetery scene, a sign writer, Arthur
Knight, had to inscribe the names and dates on some thirty
tombstones exactly as they appear in the real cemetery in
Vienna. Shrubs and trees were put into place in the mid-
distance, and Ferdinand Bellan painted a thirty-foot-long
backdrop representing the distant view of the cemetery.
    Bellan, born in Vienna, was one of the great unsung talents
of British film-making. He'd worked with Korda since the
earliest days of London Films. The producer Norman Spencer,
who had started in the industry at Denham Studios in the
1930s, remembered his work on Korda's Russian Revolution
epic *Knight without Armour*. 'There was a scene in which they
wanted a grand palace-like house with great big ancestral
portraits. Well, Bellan would knock off a couple of portraits
before lunch. And they were there for the mob to come in and

cut and slash them. They called him "scenic artist", but he would do pictures of any period at the drop of a hat.'[7] He could paint a twenty by thirty foot backing quicker than it took to make a photographic one – and with just as much verisimilitude. When Carol Reed began to work on the café scene, Bellan painted the street in which the café stood on a backing which stretched the entire width of Stage A. The street was in perfect perspective and matched the original Vienna location in every detail. It took him three days.[8]

The last scene to be filmed at the end of March was the play that Anna appears in at the Josefstadt Theatre when Holly meets her for the first time – not some classic eighteenth-century German drama, as I had always assumed, but just an isolated scene written specifically for the occasion. The shots of Martins and the audience looking on had been taken on location in the actual theatre, the unit moving in after the evening performance.

Karl Stepanek and Hannah Norbert were Anna's fellow actors in this play within a film. They were just two of the many faces that appear in *The Third Man* without any credit. With the aid of the artists' contracts which still exist in David Selznick's archives,[9] it's possible to put names to most of these people. Many of them, however briefly glimpsed, were memorable under Carol Reed's direction. The large lady whom Baron Kurtz serenades in the Casanova Club – seen on the screen for about three seconds and described in her contract as 'butcher's wife' – was Madge Brindley. The young Austrian man who asks Holly Martins at his lecture what he thinks of James Joyce was Fritz Krenn. The unforgettably cross if silent lady who is seen on three separate occasions in the company of the oleaginous Cultural Re-education officer Mr Crabbin was Paula Breeze.

The disparity of remuneration for these small parts, as for the bigger ones, is notable, and of course – in the way of such matters – bears no relation to the impact the characters actually make in the film. So Martin Miller, who played the headwaiter of the Casanova and is completely forgettable, was earning £50 a day, while the marvellous Paula Breeze earned just £6.

Compared to Vienna, shooting in Shepperton was straight-forward. No more need for Benzedrine. But even with the two units the production was running over schedule. In most circumstances Korda was happy to back Carol Reed to the hilt, but Selznick had provided Joseph Cotten and Alida Valli for fifteen and fourteen weeks respectively. After that time Korda became entirely responsible for paying their hefty salaries, and the cost of continuing the production would become exponentially more expensive.

There was also a finite limit on Cotten's services, given his need to avoid paying tax in Britain, and Selznick made sure to remind Korda of this. In December 1948, just before shooting began in Shepperton, he cabled: 'Urge you once again warn Carol that even if it means that his picture is unfinished, Cotten has to get out by the tax date because otherwise I am fearful that Carol will again count on you to get him out of what I think he regards as just minor business difficulties that you will handle with your magic wand.'[10]

Cotten's schedule was duly rearranged before shooting began in Shepperton, but he was still several weeks over schedule when he was released on 18 March, and the efforts to shoot his scenes first caused even more delays on top of those that Welles had occasioned.

At some point in the last stages of the production Korda sent in the 'broker's men', in the form of Harold Boxall and David Cunynghame, the joint managing directors of London Film Productions. Guy Hamilton remembered the morning they turned up. 'I could sense trouble because you don't often get distinguished members of London Films Board arriving unannounced . . . Korda had obviously sent them down to tell Carol to speed up or cut scenes.'[11]

Reed's tactic in such a situation was to fall back on a cultivated vagueness. He went over to greet them and then called over Hamilton, who remembers that the subsequent conversation went something like this:

'Guy, how many weeks is our schedule?'

'Sixteen, Carol.'

'How many weeks have we been shooting?'

'Fourteen, Carol.'

'How can we be over schedule if it's sixteen weeks and we've only been shooting fourteen?' he asked Cunyghame and Boxall with a look of bafflement.

When they mentioned a lengthy scene that had yet to be shot, he simply replied with uncomprehending innocence, 'What's that, Guy? Half a day. I still don't understand how can we be over schedule?'

Typically Korda did his best to avoid paying Cotten the 'overage' of salary to which he was entitled, asking him in early February if he would forego it as a 'personal favour'.[12] Cotten insisted on being paid for the time he actually worked, but grudgingly agreed to relinquish the three weeks' salary he was entitled to while he was in Paris over Christmas. But, as he explained to Jenia Reissar, he did so only 'because the picture was being made in *England*. No such concession would have been granted by him in a Hollywood picture.' He also told her that 'he was certain D.O.S. would never have asked for such a concession'.[13] Jenia Reissar then hurried to get to Alida Valli before Korda did and tell her to refuse to discuss any similar waiver. 'I think it should be made very clear to Korda that he will have to pay for the additional time with Valli and not try the stunt of getting her for nothing too.'[14] Valli's last day on the set was 31 March, which was seven weeks in addition to the original fourteen that her contract had specified. This time Korda was obliged to pay the overage in its entirety, although he didn't do so for months, pleading cash-flow difficulties.

All through the making of *The Third Man* London Films sought to ensure a maximum of publicity and a minimum of information. Newspapers were told that the film was a 'modern story of the British intelligence service', although it was not about spies at all. 'Filming is expected to begin in Vienna this winter,' reported the *New York Herald Tribune* in August 1948. 'Other locations called for in the story are London, Paris and Rome,' it added – wrongly – faithfully passing on what it had been told.

The prime advocate of such secrecy was Carol Reed. He suggested to Ingram Fraser, the publicity director of London Films, that 'without giving the impression of trying to keep the plot of the film secret, we should side-step as much as possible so that the main story is not known beforehand'.[15] He was upset when Valli let slip details of the plot during location shooting in Vienna. He worried about what would happen now that the production had moved to Shepperton Studios, where the actors would be more easily accessible to reporters. At his request, Fraser agreed 'to talk to each of them separately and suggest the line they should follow in answering interviewers' questions'.[16]

Back in London, Reed was dismayed to read a report in a trade journal which stated that Orson Welles was playing 'Harry Lime, an American racketeer'. In an irked letter to Fraser he wrote: 'If this sort of thing is going to be said even by our own studio a great deal of the surprise value of the picture will be lost.'[17] He added, 'If you feel that it is essential to give the character or what his job in Vienna is, let's make up a fictitious name and story of our own, but never mention Lime or an American racketeer.'

Today the greatest 'surprise' entrance in cinema surprises no one. Perhaps it rivals only Welles' Rosebud as the cinema's least surprising surprise. Harry's face in the doorway has an iconic status. The only surprising thing is that anyone should have thought that it would be a surprise then. Welles had carved a niche for himself by playing mysterious strangers and villains. The audience had only to see his name in the opening credits to anticipate his devilry and wait.

7

'You'll Never Teach These Austrians to be Good Citizens!'

In the film, the Austrians are a humbled people, second-class citizens in their own capital. Holly Martins has to meet Baron Kurtz in a café around the corner from the Hotel Sacher, where he's staying, because Austrians aren't allowed into the building. When Martins asks for his help in solving the mystery of Lime's death, the Baron replies, 'I am an Austrian – I have to be careful with the police.' The tarnished grandeur of the city – 'bombed about a bit' – reflects the reduced circumstances of its inhabitants. The Baron himself may possess an aristocratic lineage but must perform as a fiddler in the Casanova Club. Perhaps the ugliest woman in Vienna sits at one of the tables. His serenading of her is a grotesque if oddly exuberant parody of a more elegant time.

'You'll never teach these Austrians to be good citizens!' declares the Rumanian Popescu, when Martins tells him that the porter withheld evidence concerning Harry Lime's death, and the sentiment runs as an undercurrent through the film. 'Why, I have done things that would have seemed unthinkable before the war,' confides Baron Kurtz to Martins. *The Third Man* evokes the moral uncertainty of people who have had to co-exist with evil. Denied the luxury of self-righteousness, they are condemned to have their actions always looked upon with ambivalence and suspicion. Many of the Austrians who participated in the film would have experienced this.

Here's an American writer's account of Korda's old friend

Karl Hartl, whose studios provided facilities to *The Third Man* crew: 'In 1948 post-war Austria's struggling film industry released its first notable film, *The Angel with the Trumpet*. It starred the Nazi acting couple Attila Hoerbiger and Paula Wessely. Its director was Karl Hartl, who shortly after the Anschluss had been personally appointed by Goebbels to be production chief of the Vienna Film Industry. Although Hartl and the Hoerbigers had been making anti-Semitic films just a few years earlier, their new film depicted a Jewish family sympathetically. Their fast turnaround apparently bothered no one.'[1]

This is Hartl's own account of the appointment: 'I at first declined with the remark that I was a director and did not understand enough about organisation. Thus I hesitated for a month or two and the danger then drew nearer and nearer that Goebbels and the Propaganda Ministry would simply install a German as a temporary chief who might give the production programme a completely different and possibly political slant. We ... were all agreed that it would be better after all if one of us were to do it. And that gave me the incentive to say, "OK, then I'll have a go", and thus I became head of Wien-Film from 1938 to 1945.'[2] Hartl admitted to having to make a few propaganda films, but claimed he did all he could not to. 'Anyone who studies Wien-Film production of the time in detail will soon establish that there was hardly a single film which was not set before or about the turn of the century. The main reason for this was, of course, that in such films one had hardly or not at all to express a political belief.'

The Baron, who tells Martins of the 'unthinkable' things that the war had forced ordinary people to contemplate, was played by Ernst Deutsch. By an irony he was the one German-speaking actor in the film to be spared such moral unease. A Jew born in Prague, he had worked with Max Reinhardt and was a leading actor of the German Expressionist cinema of the 1920s, but left Berlin when the Nazis came to power in 1933. In 1938 he was forced to flee again, this time from Vienna and then Prague. He appeared on the stage in London and then on

Broadway, but spent the war years in Hollywood, where he appeared in a number of films, including *Nurse Edith Carell* (1939), *The Man I Married* (1940) and *So Ends Our Night* (1941).* He returned to Europe in 1947 to star in G. W. Pabst's *Der Prozess*, for which Pabst won a prize at the 1948 Venice Film Festival. By contrast the other actors all remained household names in Austria, and – like Hartl – continued to pursue successful film and stage careers through the seven years of German rule.

But now they were just supporting players, engaged at the last moment during the location shooting in Vienna, and their services were cheaply bought. The London Film Productions files contain details of their salaries, which in each case had to be approved by the Bank of England.[3] For six days' work – three in Vienna, and three in Shepperton – Hedwig Bleibtreu, who played Anna's landlady, received 9,000 schillers, approximately £225. A legendary star of the Burgtheater, she was the Dame Edith Evans of the Austrian stage and had just received a letter from the Mayor of Vienna on the occasion of her eightieth birthday. But her celebrity status counted for little beyond Austria's borders. Paul Hoerbiger, who played the porter, received £75 per working day. He was scheduled to work approximately fourteen days – four in Vienna, ten in Shepperton – for a total salary of £1,050. Siegfried Breuer, who played Popescu, received 36,000 schillers, approximately £900. Compare these sums to the £25,000 that Orson Welles received for playing a part not much larger than Popescu's.

The German national Erich Ponto, who played Dr Winkel, was technically an enemy alien. His engagement had to be sanctioned not only by the Bank of England but also by the Foreign Office, and an elaborate procedure observed. The fact that the Allied Powers had declared Austria 'a victim of Hitlerite aggression' in 1943 considerably reduced the paperwork in the case of the Austrian members of the cast.

---

* It was an unhappy exile. Deutsch would later comment: 'Ich werde über Jahre der Emigration nicht sprechen, ich sage Ihnen nur eines: Außer einer unheilbaren Krankheit Kann einen jungen Menschen nichts Slimmeres treffen als die unfreiwillage Emigration!'

There were three camera units in Vienna, but only the two English ones received a credit. In charge of the day unit was a veteran cameraman from the German cinema's heyday who insisted on using an old-fashioned camera that looked like a shiny box. Carol Reed used to curse the Eclair because you had to look through the film itself, which passed in front of the viewfinder and if you weren't used to it you couldn't see a thing unless the camera was running. But with it Hans Schneeberger shot one of the most famous endings in the history of the cinema – Alida Valli walking down the cemetery path, past Joseph Cotten and on out of the frame.*

Robin Lowe, an interpreter for the film crew, remembers that Schneeberger used to sit alone at breakfast-time, eating very strong garlic sandwiches. The more I found out about this forgotten name, the more it seemed to me that only Erich Von Stroheim could play him – although Schneeberger had been tall and athletic. In the First World War he had been a lieutenant in the Austrian army, and was decorated for his bravery in mountain warfare against the Italians. He was one of the best downhill skiers in Austria and an expert climber. In the twenties he worked as a cameraman on Dr Arnold Fanck's mountain films and fell in love with Dr Fanck's star, the young Leni Riefenstahl. He would reluctantly play opposite her in *The Great Leap* (1927) because no one else was capable of the acrobatic feats on skis that were required of the male lead.

His Alpine exploits earned him the nickname of 'Snowflea'. Madly in love, and sharing equal passion for adventure, cameraman and star would do anything to get the spectacular shot. One film they made together required the female lead to be engulfed in an avalanche on her way to her cabin. So they waited for bad weather before venturing out on to the Flexen Pass, where they hoped to shoot the scene. 'It had been snowing non-stop for five days,'[4] remembered Riefenstahl,

---

* Schneeberger finally received a credit in 1953 when he was the second-unit cameraman on Carol Reed's *The Man Between.*

and the Flexen Pass was blocked so that no sleigh, no horse, no human being could get through, and there was an extreme danger of avalanches. That was precisely what we needed, but we couldn't talk anyone into accompanying us. The mountain guides thought we were crazy... So we decided to do it on our own. Snowflea took the camera and the tripod while I carried the suitcases containing the camera lenses. The blizzard was so awful that we could not even see thirty feet ahead. Slowly we struggled against the storm; small and large avalanches kept rolling down from the heights. We had to locate a suitable place and find cover under overhanging boulders so that we wouldn't be swept into the chasm. The camera was set up and we waited and froze... At last we heard a roaring overhead and Snowflea leaped over to the camera, and I to the prepared place, where my hands could cling to the rock. Suddenly all was darkness, I felt the snow piling up on me, solid and heavy – I was buried! Now I really was afraid. I felt my heart hammering as I tried to push my way out with my arms, head and shoulders. Then I felt Snowflea's hands digging above me. I could breathe again.

'We got terrific shots,' he said. 'Fanck is going to be really excited.'

A quarter of a century later the war hero and skiing champion – I suppose a little like Stroheim's Max Von Mayerling in *Sunset Boulevard* – was living in obscurity, taking on any assignment he could. But it was an unexceptional story in the Vienna of those years.

8

The Fourth Man

One of the most singular strokes of good fortune was the music – the zither twang of 'The Third Man Theme' sounding like a cross between a guitar and a barrel organ. Fifty years on everyone knows it. Over 40 million copies of the tune have been sold. Everybody, from the Shadows to the Beatles, has done a cover version.

When the film opened, the music was a sensation, and the unknown zither player was hailed as the 'Fourth Man'. As an American advertisement for the film put it: 'Graham Greene created him . . . Carol Reed brought him to life . . . Alida Valli sought him . . . and Karas's music followed him wherever he went!'

The story that the papers ran, and which Reed for simplicity's sake would himself tell in interview after interview, was that he had discovered Karas busking in a café or wine garden. Actually he met him at a welcome party for the crew on the day they arrived in Vienna. The host was Karl Hartl.

With hundreds of people crammed into an elegant but confined flat, it was an awkward occasion. Reed and his British crew spoke no German, and only a few of the Austrians spoke English. It looked like being a painful evening of *Gut Abend's* and *Danker schön's* until suddenly a little man in a corner started plucking on a funny little instrument that looked like a cross between a harp and a guitar.

Carol Reed was entranced. He made inquiries to be told that it was a zither, and, waking up the next morning in the Astoria Hotel, he still had its tune in his head. 'That bloody zither, it's fabulous,' he told Guy Hamilton. 'We've got to have it in the picture. Find out the man's name.'[1]

So Hamilton rang up Mrs Hartl. 'But das ist ein zither player!' she said, astonished that he should have wanted to know who this musician was. And when he persisted, she explained, 'But you do not *know* the name of the zither player! They come with the glasses, with the catering!'

It took several weeks finally to track the zither player down to a *Heurigen* where he performed in Sievering, near the studios. A *Heurigen* was a place where wine-makers would sell the season's wine (*Heurig* meaning 'of this year'). They would advertise the new vintage by tying some twigs from the appropriate vine to the end of a pole, which they then fastened above their doors.

By this time Carol Reed was immersed in his exhausting schedule, directing three units virtually round the clock. He arranged to meet the zither player on Sunday, the only day off from shooting.

When the musician duly turned up at the Astoria Hotel at about ten o'clock in the morning, the whole crew was still asleep, catching up after their week's exertions. Carol Reed answered a knock on his hotel room door to find a little man about the size of Charlie Chaplin, who wore a rather worn suit and carried a leather briefcase. He looked more like a commuter on Waterloo Bridge than a musician, and, as Reed himself was a large man well over six feet tall, and still wearing his dressing-gown and pyjamas, the encounter must have had an incongruous aspect.

Ushering the musician in, Reed made signs to him to play his music as he had done on the night of the party. The musician sat down at a table and took his instrument out of its briefcase. It took only a few chords to convince the director that the strange music he had heard so many weeks ago and couldn't get out of his head was not a misplaced enthusiasm. He sent his assistant off to wake up the sound crew, who assembled in his bedroom with an old Klangfilm recorder, a cheap system that was used only for tests.

As the whole hotel now was beginning to wake up, they stuffed pillows and blankets underneath the doors to drown out the sound of the maids marching up and down in the corridor outside. First Karas played popular standards like 'The Blue Danube' and 'La Vie en rose'. He must have thought that this was the music that would most impress the director. But with great difficulty finally making himself understood, Reed asked him if he knew anything out of copyright. It was then that Karas began to play the music that would put most people listening to it today in mind of *The Third Man*. He played for hours, the sound crew recording him.

At this stage Carol Reed still had no idea what he was going to do with this music, he just knew he had to use it somehow. The little Austrian musician and his zither were quickly forgotten again the following day as the crew returned to their punishing shooting-schedule. It was only several weeks later, when the studio scenes were being shot in Shepperton, that Reed was at last able to address the matter.

He decided to try the music out on the Wednesday rough cut nights. He asked the editor, Oswald Hafenrichter, to lay the zither music that had been recorded in his hotel room against the silent sequences in the picture, which consisted mostly of the location footage shot in Vienna.

These Wednesday night screenings became a kind of private preview, and the sequences with the zither were somehow always the most satisfying. Reed had initially envisaged the zither as no more than incidental music to provide a sense of atmosphere, but now his thoughts moved on. 'I'll use the zither throughout the picture, but an orchestra for the chase,' Guy Hamilton remembered him saying.

But every Wednesday, as the picture grew fatter and fatter, the cutting-room added more and more music. And when they found a sad bit that they laid against the final sequence of Alida Valli walking down the cemetery path, Reed finally bowed to the might of the zither. 'Err, not symphonic, I think it will be all the way through . . .'

According to David Eady,[2] who was a cutting-room assistant on the picture, Oswald Hafenrichter played a decisive part in bringing Reed around to this way of thinking. An Austrian, who had studied medicine in Vienna before the war, he 'played all this music with tears running down his cheek'.* Asked by Reed to find some suitable music for Harry Lime's arrival at the Great Wheel, he chose the sequence which would later become famous as the 'Harry Lime Theme'.

'Why don't you use this tune throughout the film?' he suggested to Reed. 'Look, I'm not making a Wagner opera,' Reed replied. 'Just put it where I said at the meeting at the Great Wheel.' Rather than argue with him, Hafenrichter – whom Eady remembered as 'both a coward and very obstinate' – went to the sound department and got them to lay the tune very softly against the final sequence. 'I wonder what Carol will say,' he thought aloud with a hint of trepidation in his voice.

The film was run, and the final sequence played. 'The lights went up and silence,' Eady recalled. 'And Carol Reed said to Oswald, "You know, Ossie, I've been thinking, it might be a good idea to use this tune whenever Harry Lime is on the screen."'

With his zither Karas provided one of the most celebrated pieces of film music of all time. Fifty years on it's become such a treasured part of film history that it's hard to appreciate how harebrained Reed's decision must have seemed then. The forties were the great age of the orchestral film score. The big pictures, almost as a matter of course, had scores by the leading composers of the day – Walton, Vaughan Williams, Alwyn, Addinsell. To suggest using a *zither* – whatever that

---

* Hafenrichter's life followed an appealingly Quixotic path. He gave up his medical studies to become a photographer in Berlin. He then worked at UFA studios in Germany, where he edited *Mädchen in Uniform* in 1931. Throughout the 30s he was a member of the German Communist Party. As an anti-Nazi, he was several times arrested by the Gestapo. He moved on to France, where he joined the French army at the beginning of the war. He escaped to England with British troops at Dunkirk, and, after a spell in prison and then the Pioneer Corps, entered the British film industry as a projectionist. He received an Academy Award nomination for *The Third Man*, but at this high point in his career left for South America to help the ex-Ealing producer and director Alberto Cavalcanti establish a film industry in his native Brazil.

might be – was like Steven Spielberg telling John Williams not to bother turning up and hiring instead a man he'd met on the beach with a penny whistle.

It wasn't simply a question of aesthetics – vested interests were at stake. When London Films' director of music, Dr Hubert Clifford, took over the department, he gave an undertaking that he would use no other orchestra besides the Royal Philharmonic. Anton Karas may not have amounted to an orchestra, but it's easy to see how none the less the distinguished Dr Clifford might have resented the employment of someone who so challenged his idea of what film music was about. Perhaps significantly, one of the most notable critics of the zither soundtrack was Dr Clifford's predecessor at London Films, then musical director at the Rank Organisation, Muir Mathieson. 'The zither music in *The Third Man*,' he commented, 'was used with marvellous effect once or twice. It had some very dramatic chords. But when it started trying to give the impression of an orchestra it came outside its medium and became irritating.'[3]

Although Dr Clifford finally conceded that a zither it would have to be, he questioned Reed's choice of Karas. *He* could find Reed a really first-class zither player. As Guy Hamilton observed, what he was saying was 'totally right. It was as if Carol had hopped out of the metro at the Place Clichy and to the first blind beggar who was playing an accordion had said, "I want him to do the music." And anybody would say, "But Carol, he's the most awful accordion player there's ever been. We can get you accordion players with the London Symphony Orchestra." '

Reed dug his heels in. He insisted on Karas. 'But Anton Karas can't read music,' protested Dr Clifford. 'But nor can I,' replied Reed. 'I still want Anton Karas.' When it became clear that he would receive no willing cooperation from the director of music, Reed decided to take matters into his own hands.

Karas came over to London at the end of May 1949, and Reed put him up in his own house on the King's Road. He set up a moviola and taught Karas how to use it and to time his music to the picture. Every night over the next three months he brought back the rough cut of the picture from Shepperton Studios, where he had worked on it during the day. As neither Reed nor Karas could speak a word of the other's language, Reed's wife Pempie did a little bit of interpreting. But somehow these two seemed able to communicate without the need for words. Night after night Reed sat by Karas and coaxed a musical performance out of him much as previously on the set he had coaxed a dramatic one out of the actors.

Reed knew nothing about music, but he was in effect Karas's collaborator. He built the performance, gave it shape, put it together so that a man who had never seriously attempted any original compositions of his own before suddenly seemed expert. It was an achievement which in many ways resembled that of *The Fallen Idol*, in which Reed had taken Bobby Henrey, an eight-year-old boy who could not act, and moulded out of this raw material a flawless screen performance. The music took on a dramatic character of its own, commenting on the action with the world-weariness of a native of contemporary Vienna.

What both Henrey and Karas had to offer, more precious than any expertise, was spontaneity. Reed guarded this quality jealously. He kept the technicians well away from Karas and never let him go near the studios except for actual recordings.

Guy Hamilton, who had by this time moved on to another picture, remembers being summoned over to the Westrex studio, a state-of-the-art recording theatre at Shepperton. 'There was a terrible atmosphere. There was a small table. There was Karas sitting on a chair in front of a zither, and the screen. And there was Carol pacing up and down, smoking. He said, "Guy, listen to this. It's absolute shit." The Oscar-winning recording team ... were sitting behind the console sulking. They played back what Karas had just recorded. And Carol said, "It's not what we had, what we got in Vienna. It's not what we had. It's not what we got on the film." ... What we had in Vienna was Lotte Lenya. Dirty, gritty, and now it was, all of a sudden, perfect ... And the soundtrack of *The*

Third Man always made Carol cry because he never got the original dirty, gritty sound.'

When, shortly afterwards, the Chairman of British-Lion, Sir Arthur Jarratt, saw the film, he sent Reed a telegram: 'Dear Carol, saw *The Third Man* last night. Love it. I think you've got a big success there. But please take off the banjo.'[4]

Reed showed Guy Hamilton the telegram. 'They don't know a fucking thing,' he said with disgust at the breed of distributors that Sir Arthur Jarratt represented. He screwed up the piece of paper and threw it on the floor.

Hamilton retrieved the telegram, and, eighteen months later, when both the film and the music had achieved their colossal success, used it to blackmail Jarratt into giving him his first directing job.

Karas officially finished work on 3 September, the day after *The Third Man* opened in London, and returned home to his wife Kate and daughter Menkerl in Vienna. He must have thought that was that. A bit of excitement and a nice little windfall – he received 12,000 schillers for ten weeks' work (about £300) – and now it was back to eeking out a living in the *Heurigens* around Vienna.

But in the weeks that followed the film's opening he discovered to his astonishment that he was being hailed its star every bit as much as Cotten or Welles or Valli. The comments of the *Sunday Mercury*'s reviewer may have been more than usually thoughtful but they were typical of the sentiments of critics and audiences alike:

> Background music has always been a great source of argument. Generally speaking in my opinion America has exhibited poor taste with it, drowning dramatic sequences with a huge symphony orchestra and always aiming at the obvious.
> Perfect background music should be felt and not heard, yet can be outstanding when listened to divorced from the film. Great examples that come to

mind are *Things to Come* and *Hamlet*. Very rare cases have occurred and usually in comedy when special music has itself contributed simultaneously to the enjoyment of the film.

Until last week, however, I've never encountered background music which divided the attention without spoiling enjoyment, music unorthodox in choice of instrument and type of melody for the action it accompanied.

Ever since seeing *The Third Man* its whole musical accompaniment has haunted me. It is played on a zither by its composer, Anton Karas, about whom the producers are singularly silent.

To whose credit this choice of instrument lies I do not know, but I suspect Carol Reed. It was ideal for the Viennese background, arrests attention, and by its paradoxical movement at most dramatic moments heightens the tension more than any music in any film I've ever seen.[5]

If the producers had kept 'singularly silent' about Karas, probably it was because he seemed such a gamble – they privately feared that the audiences would laugh at the 'banjo-player'. It seems incredible today when the huge potential of record sales can determine the very character of a film soundtrack, but no record of Karas's music had even been planned. It was only in response to the public clamour that a record was hurriedly put into production, and released by Decca (F9235) in late October 1949, over a month after the film's opening. On the A side was 'The Harry Lime Theme', and on the reverse 'The Café Mozart Waltz'.

'Judging by the number of letters I have had asking for a recording of Anton Karas's zither background music, the public's response to the issue should be quite large,' wrote Steve Race in his review of the release for the *New Musical Express*.[6] In the event the disc sold as fast as it could be pressed – by the end of November half a million copies. This was an unprecedented achievement, but in Britain these were the days before the record charts, when the only formal measure of a tune's popularity was its sheet music sales.

'The Sensation of the Music Business,' declared Chappell's music publishers in early November. 'Ready shortly', it promised in adverts that appeared in the music press, would be a dance orchestra version of 'The Harry Lime Theme', arranged by Jimmy Lally, and a light orchestra version arranged by Geo L. Zalva. And for those who couldn't wait there was a piano solo version 'now on sale'.

'The Harry Lime Theme' entered the *Melody Maker*'s sheet music charts at number 17 on 19 November 1949, peaking at number 2 on 10 December. If these figures failed to match the volume of record sales, it simply reflected the new power of the turntable. The true measure of popularity now was not what you heard in the dance hall or on the radio but what you listened to at home.

Other acts were quick to jump on the bandwagon. In December the hastily assembled 'Café Vienna Quartet' released a Hawaiian guitar version of 'The Harry Lime Theme' on the Columbia label (DB2611). The *Gramophone* critic dismissed it as 'spurious'. 'Surely Columbia could have found another zither player to record the "The Harry Lime Theme" and "The Café Mozart Waltz"?'[7] Perhaps they should have asked Dr Clifford.

In the weeks running up to Christmas 1949 there was scarcely a band in London who didn't feature the tune in their repertoire. The Malcolm Mitchell Trio performed it during the intermission of *Castle in the Air*, a new comedy starring Jack Buchanan which opened at the Adelphi in December. 'Before going to the play,' wrote the *Melody Maker*'s critic Mike Nevard, 'I made a wager with a colleague that the Trio would play the "Harry Lime Theme". Poor lad. While I dine out, he has to stay in the office, eating sandwiches.'[8] Not even *serious* musicians were immune. 'I took my harp to a party and everyone asked me to play *that* tune,' reported the virtuoso harpist Emil Yrrah.[9] No musician, it seemed, of whatever kind,

was safe. Even the most humble mouth-organist was expected
to be able to render a version.

And all over Britain the hunt was now on for the zither. It
was that strange twilight period before the dawning of rock 'n'
roll, on the cusp of the fifties, when the young generation had
still to break away from their elders, yet sensed the possibility
of the great liberation ahead. Maybe the Karas craze was the
sign.

Bandleaders sent their assistants on frantic searches for this
fabulous new instrument that would give their act some edge.
When Ned McCrudden, tenor saxophonist with Eddie Shaw at
the Plaza Ballroom, Belfast, confided that he had played the
zither as a young boy, Shaw instructed his band to scour the
junk shops of Belfast. Eventually 'a harp-like instrument' was
found in a store room,[10] which turned out to be an old but
hardly used zither, complete with its original strings. McCrudden couldn't remember if it had actually once been his, but he
made up for any previous lack of dedication with intense
practice sessions. He was back in tune by Christmas, and,
inevitably, the highlight of the Band's Christmas show was
'The Harry Lime Theme'.

For the benefit of its readers the *New Musical Express* quoted
the definition of a zither in *The Oxford Companion to Music*:
'It consists of a wooden box, as resonator with strings, varying
in number from about 30 to 45, stretched over its surface. Of
these a few lie over a fretted board and serve to produce the
melody, the remainder being open strings, used for accompaniment. The left hand thumb "stops" the melody strings, the
right hand thumb (to which a plectrum is attached) plays
them: meanwhile the three larger fingers of the right hand
pluck the accompaniment strings. The instrument is placed on
a table or upon the knees.'[11] Liszt had been among its
admirers, and, added the *Companion*, with just a hint of
disdain, 'surprising virtuoso and even musical effects are
possible under the hands of a skilful performer'. There was
even the intriguing possibility that Nero had watched Rome

burn to the sound of one, as the zither's ancestor was clearly established as having been the three-thousand-year-old lyre.

Yet in spite of the fortune he was making for London Film Productions, Karas wasn't entitled to a penny of the sheet music and record sales. 'We will employ you to act as a Zither player to play the Zither and to provide the music to be played by you on the Zither,' stated his contract, dated 27 May 1949,[12] and it contained a waiver of copyright clause of the kind that screenwriters were routinely required to sign. It wasn't exploitation; just a complete unawareness of the commercial potential of the music. Indeed, once it had become a success, London Film Productions entered into another agreement with Karas, which entitled him to 50 per cent of the company's receipts from record and sheet music sales.

America, where the film was not released until February of 1950, had had the benefit of forewarning. Selznick himself, who was in England to witness the zither craze at first hand, sounded the alert. On 25 November 1949 he sent this excited cable to his colleague Daniel O'Shea back in Culver City:

> Cannot commence to tell you sensation caused by Karas's zither music in 'Third Man'. It is rage of England and has already sold more record copies than any other record in entire history of the record business in England. It is widest-played dance music in England ... and ads here use 'Hear Harry Lime theme' etc., in type dwarfing all other billing. It is one of those unpredictable, tremendous sensations that I cannot expect any of you to understand who have not been here. Entirely unrelated newspaper articles and editorials, even on politics, continually refer to it. Inevitably, this success will be repeated America if we are prepared for it. We should be able to make fortune out of this music.[13]

The Selznick Releasing Organization organised a competition of thirty-two top lyricists to provide words for 'The Third Man Theme'. The winner was Buddy Bernier:

> Love was always meant to be, shared by two but
>   never three
> Love is only real when hearts begin to feel, happy
>   young and free.
> If you steal a sideward glance, while you speak of
>   sweet romance
> You will live to sigh for love will pass you by . . .

And so on. 'Not the best in the world,' commented a Selznick executive, 'but it fit our title "Third Man Theme" the best.'[14] But for Selznick himself only the best would do, and, although a vocal version with Bernier's lyrics was already recorded, he ordered it to be scrapped. He tried unsuccessfully to persuade Noël Coward to write the words instead – which, since Coward was the first person to be considered for the part of Harry Lime, would have had an aptness.

The 'Selznick Releasing Organization is planning unique distribution of *The Third Man* to tie in with anticipated popularity of its background music,' announced *Variety* in January 1950 – the word 'unique' perhaps suggesting to a later age, awash with movie spin-offs from soundtrack albums to cuddly toys, an extraordinary commercial innocence.

But rival record companies were naturally keen to take advantage of the zithermania that had crossed the Atlantic well before the film, and brought out their own variations. MGM records discovered a zither player in a Viennese café in Manhattan's Upper East Side. Franz Dietschman, who had been a violinist and oboist with the Vienna Philharmonic, was swiftly signed up to perform a new tune, 'Zither Serenade (In a Dimly Lit Café)', written to order by Buddy Kaye and Guy Wood. Thousands of copies were pressed and rushed out to record stores, then suddenly embargoed when Loews Inc, which owned MGM records, realized that, as the exhibitors of the Selznick Releasing Organization, *The Third Man* would be showing in their theatres.

In America the main competition to the original Anton Karas recording came from the hugely successful dance band

Guy Lombardo and His Royal Canadians (all-time record sales of 100 million), with Don Rodney playing a guitar solo. Released in early January, their disc went to number one and became a million-seller.

According to *Billboard*, Anton Karas's 'The Third Man Theme' was the third most popular record in America in 1950, behind Patti Page's 'The Tennessee Waltz' and 'Goodnight Irene' by Gordon Jenkins & the Weavers. Guy Lombardo's 'The Third Man Theme' was at number four, providing wonderful grist for pop trivia enthusiasts. Have two different versions of the same tune ever finished next to each other in the record charts before?

When Karas had originally come over to record the soundtrack in May of 1949, Oswald Hafenrichter and Elizabeth Montagu, two German speakers, were given the job of looking after him. Elizabeth Montagu remembers his wide-open eyes when they took him to Oxford Street. Like a visitor from the East before the fall of the Iron Curtain, he was astonished by the well-stocked stores that so pointed out the drabness of home. He offered to give the entire rights to his music if they would give him some money so that he could send some things back to his family in Vienna. 'We said, "That's awfully nice, Anton, but you send them back. We don't want to take your money from you." '[15] Since they both enjoyed generous salaries from London Film Productions, they helped him out, and he bought furniture and carpets for his small Viennese flat.

As he ventured abroad again in November 1949, summoned back to London by the success of his music, his agenda was clear. 'I am a simple man and my success seems like a dream. All I want to do is to make a lot of money and then return to my family in Vienna,' he told the *New York Herald Tribune* with disarming frankness.[16] He explained how he hated leaving his wife and daughter but was determined to make enough money 'to put by for a rainy day'. All too many of his fellow citizens would have understood his attitude.

In the winter of 1949 there was no shortage of opportunities. When he began a twice-weekly engagement at the prestigious Empress Club on 16 November 1949 he was the most popular performer in Britain. On that first night the young Princess Margaret, who turned up with the American ambassador's daughter Sharman Douglas and the Hon. Peter Ward, was favoured with a special preview. 'I'm always humming this "Harry Lime Theme". Will you play it?'[17] He did – six times over the next hour and a half – and two days later, at the Royal Film Performance (*The Forsyte Saga*), performed it for the King and Queen as well. Clearly imagining the zither to be the musical equivalent of his screen performances, the star of the show, Errol Flynn, observed: 'Now every cymbal or triangle player will take heart and hope that one day he will be discovered and made famous like Karas.'[18]

Karas embarked on an exhausting sell-out tour on Britain's variety circuit. One thousand ticket-less fans had to be turned away from the De Montfort Hall in Leicester. But if his success had come as a delightful surprise, it was clear that the attendant fame did not really suit him, and he would be only too glad, once his fortune had been made, to return to a comfortable obscurity. 'The other evening I saw Karas slip into a club bar for a drink,' reported one journalist. 'Someone recognized him, called out, "Hallo, there, Anton." The little man (only 5 ft 2 ins) drew himself up with dignity. "Pleeze," he said with an air, "tonight I am incognito." '[19]

In February 1950 Karas went over to New York for the American opening of the film and then embarked on a four-month tour of the United States. He did so as the employee of Selznick's company, Vanguard. Briefing his executives on the promotion of the film, Selznick commented, 'Perhaps the most vital part of the entire plan, and the key of it, is Karas,' and he lamented the fact that they had failed to 'tie him up' before he had secured representation with the MCA agency. If *The Third Man* was to fulfil its potential to be 'the greatest thing in show business since *Gone with the Wind*', then careful coordination was required between the film and his personal appearances.

'When we overlook Karas in making these plans, we are planning on building a skyscraper on a foundation of quick sand. *It is absolutely essential that we control Karas.*'[20]

Back in Europe, Karas played for Pope Pius XII in a special Vatican audience. His travels had netted him £35,000, making him Austria's greatest individual hard currency earner. When finally he returned home in July 1950, he received a hero's welcome. The Austrian chancellor and foreign minister were among the reception party. A humble zither-player had restored some measure of pride to an impoverished but once-powerful nation.

Karas was wise enough to realise that his career as a Personality would be short and – I suppose a bit like the professional footballer buying a pub – used the earnings from the film and his recordings to buy a bar, called – naturally – 'Der Dritte Mann'. Elizabeth Montagu remembered attending a show there the next time she visited Vienna. 'There'd be dead silence, a roll of drums, and Karas would suddenly appear all dressed up and play "The Third Man Theme" ... He was the Great Man. He would just play the tune very sort of serious – the only tune. Then everybody would clap very much and he'd do it again. Then he would go away. He was a great star.'[21]

But he never forgot his benefactor, Carol Reed, with whom he remained great friends for years to come. One of his very few original compositions after *The Third Man* was 'The Karol Theme', which he dedicated to the director.[22] And when he built his wine bar, Guy Hamilton remembered, 'the one thing that Anton insisted upon was that it had a guest room for Carol Reed and Pempie, but more important that it had a bed that was not Viennese but was six-foot-six long, and that was his pride and joy, so that Carol could come and stretch in the bed when he went to Vienna.'[23]

In the years that followed Karas would play the haunting tune of 'The Third Man Theme' only occasionally – perhaps most poignantly at Carol Reed's funeral in 1976.

9

Falling Out

Reed's painstaking collaboration with Anton Karas on the music meant that the post-production phase of the film had been an unusually lengthy one. Even if it had been clear that the film was going to be exceptional, Korda could not have looked forward to showing it to Selznick, given his capacity for interference and the fact that he was entitled under their agreement to demand retakes. Nevertheless, he urged that Selznick should see the film as soon as possible, so that Carol Reed might incorporate any necessary changes in time to enter the film for the Cannes Festival in September.[1]

Selznick came over to London in July. He was going to see the film on the 26th, but was told that Reed wasn't quite ready. Then fate intervened. The very next day he cabled back to California: 'Our bad luck apparently not over. Korda has just advised me there was studio fire last night and six reels of rough cut *Third Man* destroyed necessitating delay of two to four weeks in my seeing it.'[2]

The cutting-room had to rush to put the film back together again in time for the festival. Many people worked around the clock and extra editors were drafted in to help. 'Carol wanted to cancel the entry into Cannes,' remembered Noreen Best, one of the cutting-room staff, but Hafenrichter insisted that the film could be reassembled in time. Reed must have worried that this last-minute haste would undermine his work, but he entered into the spirit, bringing Anton Karas along to play the zither while the editors worked late into the night. 'We all loved the zither,' commented Noreen Best, 'it kept us awake.'

Probably this fire was just another coincidence, but it's difficult not to feel just a little suspicious. For there were two copies of the rough cut. Carol Reed had the second one, which he and Anton Karas used when they were working together on the music. So Selznick could easily have seen that one. If Korda had wanted to delay Selznick's viewing of the film, it wouldn't have been the first time he had resorted to such acts of God. Back in the 1930s when Korda's mammoth production of *I, Claudius* was heading for disaster, a timely car accident, almost certainly 'arranged', had resulted in Merle Oberon pulling out and the picture being scrapped. Korda was able to claim the insurance (from the Prudential, who had financed the production in the first place). It was actually a term of Korda's agreement with Selznick that he should deliver a rough cut, but the fire provided a convenient excuse to waive this obligation. Whatever, Korda would have figured that the later Selznick saw the film, and the closer it was to its final state, the less likely he would be to ask for retakes, whose cost Korda would have had to bear alone.

A month later Selznick finally did see the film. He pronounced it 'superb'. Before he had even left the screening room, Korda seized the moment to ask him as a personal favour to approve the film without asking for any retakes or additional scenes. Over the previous year and a half of their partnership Selznick's attitude to Korda had been one of habitual suspicion, but now he let down his guard. In a cable to Reissar he commented: 'Think this is time when we can afford to deal with him graciously.' The contract had stipulated that the negative would be delivered to the Selznick Releasing Organisation in Culver City, California. Now he agreed to allow it to stay for the time being in England so that Carol Reed could participate in the amendments that were needed for the American version. It was a decision that he would come to regret.

On 2 September 1949 *The Third Man* opened to rave reviews in London, and Selznick returned by boat to New York with a print of the film. Anxious that it should open in America as soon as possible, he arranged for a preview to take place in New Rochelle, just a short distance north of New York City. The cards with the audience responses were then airmailed west and broken down into a report that was ready for him when he arrived back in California a few days later. The reactions of the New Rochelle audience provided the basis for his re-edited version of the film. It didn't matter how much Selznick liked the film himself or respected the artistic judgement of Carol Reed; it didn't even matter that people were now flocking to see *The Third Man* in London – an American audience would finally decide what the American audience would see.

Selznick had also to cater for the more traditional form of censorship. In the course of the production the Motion Picture Association of America had had their say. Now it was the turn of the Catholic Legion of Decency, whose approval was just as important for the success of the picture. By the time Selznick was ready to begin editing on Monday 12 September, he knew that their only major objections were the presence of a sparsely clad dancer in a nightclub scene, and the appearance of a priest at the funeral of a 'morally objectionable character' who has not expressed repentance – i.e. Harry Lime. While the first point was easy enough to meet with a simple cut, one of Selznick's executives, Bob Gillham, was left to argue the second with the Legion. 'I expect to work on them on basis of Graham Greene as one of their prize converts would not knowingly write the script without having in mind the fact that Welles repented in the end.'[3]

Now that Selznick was editing the Western Hemisphere version, he had to settle the issue of billing. 'Of course my name will come first,' he stated in a memorandum on the matter.[4] A more notable decision was to agree to a concession that Alexander Korda had asked for back in February. Trevor Howard was a big star in Britain, but hardly known at all in America, where *Brief Encounter* had done well in a few of the smaller city theatres but attracted just a fraction of the audience Selznick hoped for *The Third Man*. Korda wanted Howard to have a feature credit in the American release, although Selznick was under no contractual obligation to grant him this. His decision none the less to do so reveals the enormous degree to which his concept of *The Third Man* had changed. 'I want to co-star Trevor Howard, not merely as a courtesy and favor,' he commented, 'but because I think it makes the picture very much more important not to give it the limitations of a Cotten–Valli vehicle.' Welles, it is true, was also to enjoy a feature credit from the outset, but in Selznick's opinion that was of very little account. 'I don't think this trio of stars any more important than just Cotten and Valli, except for prestige purposes.' It was the presence of a fourth star who had yet to blot his copybook at the box office, Trevor Howard,* that made the difference and helped to take the film 'out of the category of a two-star vehicle'.

Selznick's increased sense of the importance of the film also caused him to give the title he had once wanted to change a greater prominence. 'I should like to use the names of the four stars *under* the title.' But in this he was merely following what Korda had already decided to do as a matter of course on the English version. Here was the difference between a more literary British cinema and a Hollywood that tended to think almost exclusively in terms of the box-office currency of stars.

But Selznick had been the producer who brought a young Hitchcock over from Britain and turned him into one of the very few directors whose name could compete with the stars. He clearly hoped to do the same with Carol Reed. He had bought the rights to Reed's previous film, *The Fallen Idol*, which his company was going to promote in tandem with *The Third Man*, and was also negotiating a participation in Reed's next film for Korda. He reminded his colleagues 'of the great help that a big campaign on Reed' would have to Reed's future pictures 'which we hope and expect to have'.[5] But all his great

---

* The fee for Howard's services was, relatively, a bargain – £7,500 (roughly a quarter of what Korda had paid for Welles).

plans would be derailed by a spectacular and probably inevitable falling-out.

After Selznick saw the film at the end of August a kind of Indian summer followed in his relations with his British partners. The general cordiality was further encouraged by the film's triumphant opening the next month in London and soon afterwards its winning the Grand Prix in Cannes. But the old atmosphere of suspicion and rancour soon returned.

Graham Greene took advantage of the limelight to tell anyone who would listen that working with Selznick had been a farce. His comments got back to Selznick, who instructed Jenia Reissar to write to him. Her letter, dated 17 October 1949, was as follows:

> Dear Mr Greene,
> Mr Selznick tells me that since the opening of *The Third Man* a spate of comments have been reaching him, allegedly expressing opinions you had voiced about his interference with the script.
> Mr Selznick finds it hard to believe that you would have made any derogatory remarks:-
> Firstly, because you were fully aware of his contractual rights regarding script approvals before you went over to America for the story conferences.
> Secondly, because his impression was that you had participated in these conferences in a genuinely friendly spirit.
> Incidentally, stories of this type – allegedly originating with you – were told to me when I was in Rome last year and you were in Capri. Knowing the Italian aptitude for misquoting, I ignored them.
> I now feel, however, that since your name is being used so widely you should be told about it. I hope it is being used unjustifiably.
> Sincerely yours,
> Jenia Reissar[6]

Graham Greene replied by return:

Dear Miss Reissar,
  I suggest that you tell Mr Selznick that he should
pay as little attention to these stories as I pay to the
American stories that Mr Selznick was responsible for
writing the script of *The Third Man*.
  Yours sincerely,
  Graham Greene[7]

But far worse was to come. Selznick planned to release *The Third Man* in America as 'A Selznick Picture'. On 19 October Korda sent Selznick the following cable: 'Don't you think it is a mistake to put your American trademark on our films? While I don't dispute your right to do so I feel that it is really misleading the public into thinking that these pictures are produced in Hollywood by your company. Don't you think that a truer statement of fact would be more useful and less open to criticism?'[8]

Selznick's response was to instruct Jenia Reissar to have a 'frank and tough talk with him even by telephone or by mail saying that I am appalled and disappointed by his antagonistic attitude'.[9] He spelt out the detail of what she was to say, but helpfully allowed her some latitude: she could decide herself whether to adopt a tone of 'hurt and bewilderment on my part or one of annoyance and outrage'. He regarded the proposed exchange as just one more routine dealing with a miscreant business partner, little realising that he was about to reap the whirlwind.

A few days later Reissar duly sent her letter. In it she pointed out that the Selznick trademark to which Korda objected was not only in the contract but was also a condition made by the banks when the deal was negotiated. 'Our trademark is worth a great deal,' she continued, 'as you yourself must know from the Continent where great use of Mr Selznick's name is being made by your own distributors in their negotiations with exhibitors for *Third Man* and *Gone to Earth*.'* Neither *The*

---

* The only other Korda–Selznick production surviving from the original agreement to make four films.

Third Man nor *The Fallen Idol* could seriously be mistaken for Hollywood pictures, she argued, as so much emphasis had been placed in the promotion of these films on the fact that they were directed by Carol Reed. Then, availing herself of a tone that had less hurt or annoyance than it did piousness, she declared:

> I hope you will remember that voluntarily and out of personal friendship for you, Mr Selznick has kept your name on both the pictures, which he did not have to do . . . This was done despite the protests from our own Sales Organisation, who felt that we were stressing far too much the English origin of the pictures, and consequently taking a big financial risk . . .
>
> The use of your trademark in America would cost us a fortune, for reasons which require no explanation. Mr Selznick is sorry but he is unable to make any financial sacrifices to accommodate your desire to secure more credit than has been given, now that both pictures look like being successful.[10]

The reasons which required no explanation were that Korda's recent, extremely expensive productions (*Anna Karenina, An Ideal Husband* and *Mine Own Executioner*) had been big flops both in America and Europe, disposing distributors to look with suspicion on new Korda films. But for Reissar to state this so baldly displayed an incredible lack of tact which served no one's interests – except Korda's.

It was ironic that the practical purpose of the letter had been to offer a concession – Selznick was willing, 'out of a gesture of friendship', to advertise the film as 'A Selznick Release' instead of 'A Selznick Picture'. For now Korda used the letter as a pretext to break off relations with Selznick and to force a renegotiation of their agreement to his favour. Just as Selznick had once threatened to stop Valli from travelling to Europe until he got his way, Korda now made use of an even more valuable hostage – the negative of *The Third Man,* which

Selznick had so helpfully left in London. First he replied to Reissar's letter – although not to the puppet but to the puppeteer:

Dear David,

I enclose copy of a letter I have received from Miss Reissar. I have seldom read a stupider or ruder letter. It is full of fishwifely insinuations for which I do not blame Miss Reissar, as I am certain that the insinuations and the rudeness come to her on the telephone or in one of your voluminous cables to be transmitted to me.

However, I cannot leave the letter unanswered, nor do I propose to enter into a long correspondence with Miss Reissar, so I shall write to you instead.

After long discussions we decided to make a business deal together. I had a long talk with you and I begged you to forego your customary toughness and meanness in concluding a business deal with me and to try to make it on a friendly basis and to behave with that sense of moderate generosity and gentlemanliness which is the basis of civilized life.

In return, I promised you that I would do my best at all times to regard our connection as something different from the ordinary deals in the film industry, and to base it on the old and very sincere affection I feel towards you, rather than on simple self-interest of the moment.

Shortly after concluding this deal, you found yourself in great difficulties and you had to remake a greater part of the deal. I could have been very tough with you then. You were at the mercy of the contract you had signed, I could have asked for my pound of flesh. I did not do so. On the contrary, I let you off easily, as I had not forgotten the promise I had given you. I was dealing with a friend and not with a business associate alone.[11]

Korda's tone is so assured and persuasive that it requires an effort of will not to fall right in behind him and dismiss the overbearing Selznick instantly. But if Selznick tried never to let the personal interfere with business, Korda made it a principle to bring the two together whenever he could. The 'favours' he bestowed upon his 'friends' in business were rarely just acts of simple kindness, no sooner granted than forgotten, but rather carefully accumulated credits to be put away for future use.

None the less Selznick was such a conceited oaf that there's a satisfaction in seeing him so ruthlessly put down, and few people could have done it with as much wit and spite as Korda:

> Of course I reject with contempt the arguments which you have put to me through your Miss Reissar ... I did not ask you, by the way, to use my trademark in America. It was a foregone conclusion that you would want to use your own. But, surely there was nothing against asking a friend whom I had done a great and valuable service, to take care that my name is either completely taken off or not abused by complete silence, where the advertising of the film is concerned. Of course, this would require some thinking, and while you think a great deal, you very seldom think of anybody but yourself.

In a three-page letter that was perhaps the closest he came to rivalling Selznick's cables, Korda went on to take him to task for suggesting that London Film Productions should want to exploit the Selznick name:

> Nobody in my organisation needs the use of your name. You grossly over-rate the significance of your name on the Continent and I suppose grossly underestimate the value of mine. You should instruct your letter-writers to desist from this type of remark. *The Third Man* and *Gone to Earth* are not sold as Selznick pictures anywhere in the world. They are sold as products of London Film Productions – which

they are. It is perfectly infantile to think that my
salesmen or associates abroad, who have the same
personal loyalty to myself, perhaps mistakenly, will go
out of their way to try and sell my films with your
name alone.

Korda ended the letter with this short paragraph: 'Now,
because of Miss Reissar's letter, I feel something ugly has
happened to something good and decent. I felt a deep
friendship for you and now I feel it has been spoilt.'*

It took two weeks instead of the usual two seconds for
Selznick to think up a reply to Korda's letter, its length as usual
making up for the scarcity of wit – ten single-spaced pages.
The gist was simple: Selznick considered their friendship
terminated too, and a business deal was a business deal. 'It was
a completely arm's length transaction, in which you traded
your best for everything you could get, and in which we did
the same.'[12]

Korda now refused to deliver the negative of *The Third
Man*, although Selznick's lawyers quickly conceded all the
points that had initially caused the dispute. The film would be
a Selznick 'release', not 'picture', Korda would have a personal
credit and also the right to have his name on advertising.
Korda simply alleged that the Selznick Releasing Organisation
had been responsible for other breaches of contract, which had
to be resolved first, although he did not specify what they
were.

In a statement prepared for his lawyers on 26 November,
Selznick commented, 'I can only think that there must be
motives that do not meet the eye for Sir Alexander's
unprecedented behaviour.'[13] It was an uncharacteristically
veiled remark. The reason for Korda's behaviour was obvious.
The Third Man was breaking box-office records all over
Europe. If it performed in America on the same scale, Selznick
had estimated that it would gross a colossal – for the time –

---

* To Selznick's fury Korda was still able to invite Selznick's wife, Jennifer Jones, to
dinner a few days later. She wisely declined to attend.

6–8 million dollars, but Korda wasn't entitled to a cent of this. What had seemed like a good bargain back in May 1948, assigning the Western Hemisphere rights in return for the American stars and finance, must have seemed like a lousy one now. But all was not lost so long as he had the negative.

The situation brings to mind Korda's famous retort when the British producer Michael Balcon protested, 'But Alex, we had a gentlemen's agreement' after some undertaking had been wriggled out of. 'Ah, but Mickey,' he replied, 'you need two gentlemen for that!' Selznick on more than one occasion maintained that Korda had privately admitted his tactic.[14] This would have been entirely in character.

While the lawyers fought it out, Korda reverted to his usual good humour. 'In spite of everything I appreciate and thank you for your generous food packages,' he cabled Selznick on 28 November.* 'Wish your generosity would extend to other things as well.'[15]

Selznick had planned that the film would open in Los Angeles on 23 November 1949. This was now cancelled and plans for the American release put on hold while Selznick production staff made efforts to ascertain if a dupe negative could be made from an English print. 'The print we have is bad qualitywise,' came the reply, 'the usual English lab work.'[16] But at least it provided a pretext to let off steam against perfidious Albion. Even Selznick, who certainly couldn't criticise the film itself, would indulge in these sorts of remarks. The dubbing levels were 'sloppy', the dialogue was 'rubbery' and the dissolves were 'second rate' and 'chalky'.[17]

As the wrangle continued into the new year, clumsy attempts were made to turn Carol Reed against Korda. One can only marvel at Selznick's hopeless psychology given the fact that Korda in the past – then much to Selznick's disapproval – had always given Reed the most unwavering

---

* These food parcels, which Selznick dispatched to Carol Reed and Graham Greene too, contained luxuries like ham and chocolate which were still rationed in England. They seem to have been one of the major attractions of the deal.

support. In a cable dated 5 January 1950 Selznick told Reed that the delay had ruined the chances of Karas, Krasker, Greene and Welles winning Academy Awards. He went on:

> I also had secret hope of not only picture and directorial awards but also Thalberg Award to you for both films [i.e. *The Third Man* and *The Fallen Idol*] which presented extraordinary opportunity now probably forever lost of two magnificent films from you in one year, but of course Korda has made all this impossible. I have not slightest objection your showing him this cable or in fact inviting him to challenge it. Korda himself admitted that his actions were confessedly designed to acquire a drastic change in his contracts with me and to force me to pay him huge sums from American releases for which he had not bargained at the outset . . .
>
> I freely concede that Korda is succeeding in harming *Third Man* by delaying its release. I am now all set to release although later than I planned. As to damage Korda is causing me the amount is mounting daily. It seems extremely unfair that your position and prestige should also be damaged but I am most eager for you to understand that any impossibility on my part of carrying through your every preference as to both handling of music and cutting and dubbing of picture itself is directly traceable to Korda.[18]

Reed – a much better psychologist – was careful to adopt a stance of conciliatory even-handedness. He cabled back: 'Assure you Korda has success of picture just as much at heart as you or me. My only hope is that you two will settle your differences as I cannot believe that either you or Korda are one hundred per cent right against each other.'[19] Two weeks later, unable to come to New York to collect the prestigious Critics' Award, he asked Selznick to accept it on his behalf. It was the sort of ploy he would occasionally use to win the trust of a particularly difficult actor. He would be a lot less generous about Selznick in later years when he no longer had to deal with him.

Korda knew he could keep the American release of *The Third Man* entangled in legal obfuscations for months if necessary, and that Selznick would want to settle quickly rather than put at risk a probable box-office bonanza. The film had to be released sooner rather than later to take advantage of the huge momentum of publicity that had been generated in Europe. An agreement was duly hammered out. Korda got the participation in the American receipts that he had wanted, and the film finally opened in New York in February.

Korda and Selznick may have made up, but they probably knew even before the dispute that they would never work together again. 'I was sitting with them about two years after the picture had opened,' Orson Welles recalled many years later, 'when all Europe was still reverberating with the strains of "The Third Man Theme", and Alex said, "You know, David, I hope I don't die before you do." "Oh!" said David. "Why?" And Alex said, "I hate the thought of you sneaking out at night and scratching my name off the tombstone." '[20]

10

From Fool to Hero

It's impossible to imagine that Carol Reed would have been pleased with the American version of the film. One of the regrets of the Selznick–Korda dispute was that it had prevented Reed from having any say in Selznick's re-editing of the film for the American market, although of course his opinion was always going to count for less than those of the preview audience in New Rochelle.

The chief difference between the British and American versions was Selznick's attempt to turn Holly Martins into the hero that he had always wanted him to be. In the British version Carol Reed's voice narrates the opening documentary images of contemporary Vienna:

> I never knew the old Vienna before the war with its Strauss music, its glamour and its easy charm. Constantinople suited me better. I really got to know it in the classic period of the black market. We'd run anything if people wanted it enough – mmm – had the money to pay. Of course a situation like that does tempt amateurs. But, well, you know, they can't stay the course like a professional. Now the city, it's divided into four zones, you know, each occupied by a power, the American, the British, the Russian and the French. But the centre of the city, that's international, policed by an international patrol, one member of each of the four powers. Wonderful. What a hope they had, all strangers to the place, and none

of them could speak the same language, except a sort of smattering of German. Good fellows on the whole, did their best you know. Vienna doesn't really look any worse than a lot of other European cities, bombed about a bit. Oh, I was going to tell you, wait, I was going to tell you about Holly Martins, an American. Came all the way to visit a friend of his. The name was Lime. Harry Lime. Now Martins was broke and Lime had offered him some sort, I don't know, some sort of a job. Anyway there he was, poor chap, happy as a lark and without a cent.

UGH

This is just about my favourite opening to a film. I love the conceit of the disembodied voice that belongs to some unnamed racketeer we never meet. It has a spontaneous, inconsequential quality. It could be a story, you know, told in a bar, a story as easily not told. 'Oh, I was going to tell you, wait, I was going to tell you . . .' Affable and engaging, we fall for the charm of this voice so clearly on the wrong side of the moral divide, as people must have fallen for Harry Lime. With its Old World cynicism it sets up Holly Martins as the New World innocent, out of his depth. He's the kind of amateur mentioned, who might easily end up face down in the Danube, but doesn't realise the trouble he's heading into. Within seconds of our first meeting him he's shrugged off the failure of his friend to meet him at the station and blithely walked under a ladder. He's too confident, too neglectful of chance.

But what would Selznick have made of it? Probably, to judge by the script conferences, he would have objected that nothing was established and there was no continuity. Who was that voice at the beginning? And what was that nonsense about 'we'd run anything'? Who's 'we'? And what does Constantinople have to do with anything?

Selznick simply changed it the way he wanted it to be. Problems of continuity were solved at a stroke by making the voice Holly Martins. Here's the American opening as narrated by Joseph Cotten:

I never knew the old Vienna before the war with its
Strauss music, its glamour and its easy charm. I really
got to know it in the classic period of the black
market. They could get anything if people wanted it
enough. Of course a situation like that does tempt
amateurs. But you know of course they don't last
long, not really, not like professionals. Now the city's
divided into four zones, you know, American, British,
Russian and the French. But the centre of the city,
that's international, policed by an international patrol,
one member of each of the four powers. Wonderful.
You can imagine what a chance they had, all of them
strangers to the place, and no two of them speaking
the same language. But they were good fellows on the
whole and did their best. Vienna doesn't look any
worse than a lot of other European cities, bombed a
little of course. Anyway, I was dead broke when I got
to Vienna. A close pal of mine had wired me offering
me a job doing publicity work for some kind of a
charity he was running. I'm a writer, name's Martins,
Holly Martins. Anyway down I came all the way to
old Vienna happy as a lark and without a dime.

Now everything is established, and all mystery eliminated, as
Holly Martins takes control of his own story. The worldly
unknown British voice with a dubious past becomes the
known and down-to-earth American one. You can't imagine
Holly Martins ever having been within a million miles of
Constantinople. Oklahoma suited him better. A startling,
offbeat and ironic beginning becomes a humourless and
conventional opening to a Hollywood thriller, with no more
purpose than to establish the scene. Everything is just what it
is. To Holly Martins the military police in Vienna really are
'good fellows on the whole doing their best'. The ambiguity
and delicious mischief of the original are lost. Anything
irregular or slightly irreverent is straightened out. The
insouciant understatement of 'bombed about a bit' becomes
the prosaic 'bombed a little of course'. Even the casual,

conversational tone now seems false. For there's nothing spontaneous about the introduction now, it's just the hero telling his story.

The British introduction opens up the imagination; the American one closes it down. The changes are very small – just the odd rephrasing here and there, a few words cut – but they reflect the vast gulf between British irony and the Hollywood need for clarity and reassurance. In the American version you know that Martins is going to be around in the end. In the British one, there's every possibility that he might not be.

The changed opening set the tone for the kind of snips Selznick would make throughout to give Holly Martins a bit of backbone. After Harry's funeral, Major Calloway buys a shocked and maudlin Holly Martins a few drinks:

> MARTINS: I guess nobody knew Harry like he did . . . like I did.
> CALLOWAY: How long ago?
> MARTINS: Back at school. I was never so lonesome in my life until he showed up.
> CALLOWAY: When did you see him last?
> MARTINS: September '39.
> CALLOWAY: When the business started? See much of him before that?
> MARTINS: Once in a while. Best friend I ever had.

In the American version Holly says, in one go, 'I guess nobody knew Harry like he did . . . like I did. Best friend I ever had.' The brief details of their past are removed. The amendment corrected an obvious inconsistency. Holly and Harry are meant to be Americans. The reference here to 'September '39' was an oversight. In the final draft of the script they had been portrayed as Canadian to explain why they were subject to British authority in Vienna. But Selznick insisted that they should be American. So now this cut finished a task that had been incompletely carried out, but it also undermined – or corrected – the rather forlorn and vulnerable figure that

Greene and Reed had intended. Nothing now about Holly's loneliness at school. A dimension, ever present, in Greene's novels – the way the past marks a person – was suppressed.

At Police Headquarters, after confiscating her passport, Major Calloway asks Anna to help him with information about Harry Lime. 'What can I tell you but you've got everything upside down,' she replies. He wearily dismisses her, realising that his request has been futile: 'OK ... That American friend of yours is still waiting for you. He won't do you much good. Thank you, Miss Schmidt, we'll send for you when we want you.' The American version cuts out the line, 'He won't do you much good'. There's a clumsy jump, but it was an essential change, for the thing about American heroes is that they are supposed to do lots of good. 3

Major Calloway plainly thinks Martins is a fool, and the American version has to curb him a second time. In an empty night-time square Martins tells a disbelieving Calloway that he's just seen Harry Lime alive. 'You don't think I'm blind, do you!' 'Yes!' retorts the Major, who has to accept that apparently Lime just vanished into thin air. But then he notices Lime's escape route – an advertising kiosk which leads down to the sewers. As he opens a door in its side he comments, 'It wasn't the German gin.' The line was cut out, 4 presumably because of its suggestion of Martins' habitual drunkenness.

The biggest amendment Selznick made in this programme of rehabilitation occurs when, in a railway café, Martins admits to Anna that he is going to help the police catch Harry. In a long dialogue exchange Anna calls him a liar as at first he skirts the truth of what he has agreed to do. It's the point in the film at which Holly appears most craven and guilt-ridden, and Selznick removed a long dialogue sequence even though it resulted in a severe disruption of continuity: one moment 5 Holly is wearing a coat, the next just a jacket; one moment Anna is wearing her coat alone, the next she has another coat on top. The explanation denied to American audiences lay in the cut footage: Holly had given Anna his coat to wear on the cold train.

These attempts of Selznick to redeem Holly were futile and finally irritating because they go so against the grain of Holly's character, firmly established in the substance of the film.

Selznick's other changes were superficial tinkering no doubt intended to meet concerns raised by the New Rochelle preview. When Holly meets Baron Kurtz at the Café Mozart, he inquires about Harry's girlfriend. There's the following dialogue exchange:

> BARON KURTZ: You oughtn't to speak to her. It would only cause her pain.
> MARTINS: Not necessarily. She'd probably want to help.
> KURTZ: What's the good of another post mortem? Suppose you dig up something – well, discreditable to Harry?

These lines were cut probably because they were thought to undermine the surprise of Holly's friend turning up later very much alive as the great villain of the piece.

After Major Calloway has run through the evidence that proves Lime to be a racketeer, Martins drowns his sorrows at a cheap nightclub. In the British film we briefly see a near-naked dancing girl. She was cut out of the American version, as we have already seen, because of the objections of the Catholic Legion of Decency, although curiously she resurfaces in one of the American trailers for the film.

Selznick even tinkered with Harry's appearance in the doorway. Leaving Anna's flat, Martins realises that he is being watched. 'What kind of a spy do you think you are, satchel-foot? What are you tailing me for? Cat got your tongue? Come on out, come out, come out whoever you are.' All this is the same, but then the American version omits a shot of the cat sitting at the stranger's feet and a line of dialogue – 'Step out in the light and let's have a look'. Perhaps it was felt that this mention of stepping out into the light too much anticipated the beam of light that finally does reveal the stranger's identity.

The most crass change was made for the sake of narrative clarity. After Lime has been spotted alive, the police return to the cemetery to dig up his grave. The British film shows the men digging. Then Major Calloway looks down into the open coffin, which the audience does not see, and identifies the body as that of Joseph Harbin. Selznick's version of this scene opens with a close-up of a shovel clearing the earth from the coffin lid to reveal the words HARRY LIME, just in case anyone had forgotten who was supposed to have been buried there. This crudity was particularly unfortunate for being so completely at odds with Carol Reed's elliptical style of direction.

So much of the filmic brilliance of *The Third Man* lies in what is suggested rather than shown. The only excuse for some of Selznick's interventions is that he just didn't understand what he was spoiling. A great scene – ruined in the American version – is Holly Martins' visit to a children's hospital. Major Calloway takes him there so that he can witness the damage that Harry Lime has done.

We are shown Martins' expression as he walks along a row of hospital beds, we are shown the nurses dispensing care, but neither see nor hear a single child. It's as if their lives, reduced nearly to zero, are too tenuous to make their presence felt. Attached to a child's bed at which Calloway and Martins briefly stand is a teddy-bear. It is glimpsed again at the end of the scene, as it is dumped by a nurse into a box, a symbol of one more murdered child and all the broken young lives.

This teddy-bear is perhaps the more effective for being an almost hackneyed image. It brings home the truth that Major Calloway manipulates sentiment – as single-mindedly as any Hollywood director – to persuade Martins to help him. Earlier on that day, in the Great Wheel high above Vienna, Martins had asked Harry if he had ever seen any of his victims.

'Victims?' he replied, 'Don't be melodramatic,' and pointed to the dots on the ground far below.

The teddy-bear counterbalances the dots. It comes to represent not just the victims of Harry's evil, but our humanity, and our ability to feel. In the American version we just glimpse the bear being thrown into the box. Its first key appearance and an accompanying line of dialogue from Calloway are left out: as the two visitors look at the child to whom the teddy-bear, visible in the foreground, belongs, Calloway comments, 'It had meningitis. They gave it some of Lime's penicillin. Terrible pity, isn't it?' A silent reproach lies behind Calloway's words and his emotional blackmail becomes clear. The absence of these few seconds of footage mars the whole scene.

When, a little while ago, the American Film Institute conducted a poll of the top 100 American films, *The Third Man* was voted as number 57. But had the voters *really* seen *The Third Man*? Not if it was Selznick's re-edited version that they had in mind. You can't help wondering how the original un-doctored film – the British version – would have fared in the poll? Would it have gone up? Or down?

11

'Pardon Me If I Rave!'

The Third Man opened at the Plaza, Piccadilly on Friday 2 September 1949 at what was a particularly propitious time for a film set in Vienna. The exhibition 'Art Treasures from Vienna', which was in its last week at the Tate Gallery, had attracted enormous interest. Over a quarter of a million people attended, even though the exhibition was – as *The Times* put it – 'one with not a negligible entrance fee' (1s. 6d.).[1]

The acclaim for the film was near-unanimous. Its rare feat was to unite both the high-brow critics and the pundits of the popular papers. 'Karas's improvisations, Graham Greene's characters and dialogue, and Carol Reed's narrative skill with camera, actors, and background form a collaboration of genius,' declared William Whitebait of the *New Statesman.*[2] 'Pardon Me if I Rave!' ran the *Daily Mirror* headline, praising the film for combining 'superb artistry' with '100 per cent entertainment value'.[3]

Within days of its West End opening so many special prerelease showings had been arranged up and down the country that the prefix 'pre' didn't really mean very much. Pasted into Carol Reed's cuttings book are the reviews of the nationals but also countless local newspapers: 'The people of Felixstowe are much to be envied,' began a review in the *Ipswich Evening Star,*[4] which – unusually lucid, perceptive and heartfelt – deserves to be quoted at length:

They have this week at the Ritz Cinema a pre-release
showing of the new Carol Reed film, *The Third
Man* . . .

. . . The construction is so skilled, the tension so
well sustained one cannot tear one's eyes away from
the screen.

I am a heavy smoker, but I could not find the time
to light a cigarette.

I have only experienced this once before in the
cinema at a film called *The Tunnel,* made by a British
company with Richard Dix in 1935. But I was young
then, more easily pleased, and I had hardly started
smoking.

Film making is such a team business it is difficult
to tell who exactly is responsible for what. Who for
instance first suggested that the background music be
provided by a zither? Composed and played by Anton
Karas, this music, with its haunting, recurring theme,
adds immensely to the film and brilliantly points its
mood, a mood of pitying sadness, which is inherent
in all the work of Graham Greene.

The Third Man is a major triumph for all
concerned, but chiefly for its director Carol Reed,
who needs your sympathy in that he now has to
follow it up. Reed is not only a superlative craftsman
and the great white hope of British pictures, he is also
a visual genius.

His films, and none more than this, are packed
with images, all of which help to tell the story, by
adding to its depth and meaning. They invariably
contain that extra 10 per cent of care, thought and
imagination, which would, if only it were more
widespread, so certainly turn the tide in the affairs of
the British film industry.

Please remember *The Third Man.* Please tie a knot
in your handkerchiefs and when it comes your way
do not fail to see it. It is one of the curses of the
film world that superlatives are too lightly thrown
about, but I say in all seriousness that this is the
finest film I have ever seen.

Two weeks after its opening in London *The Third Man* appeared at the Third Cannes International Film Festival. Britain's other three entries were the Ealing comedy *Passport to Pimlico*, David Lean's *Passionate Friends* and Thorold Dickinson's excellent *Queen of Spades*. The rich and famous visitors that year included the Duke and Duchess of Windsor, the Aga Kahn, Jean-Paul Sartre and Jean Cocteau. But the great talk of the festival was the romance between Orson Welles' ex-wife Rita Hayworth and the millionaire Aly Khan.

The film won the first ever overall Grand Prix of the Festival. In the previous two years prizes had been awarded by categories. *France-Soir* devoted a special issue to its victory. 'Sur le plan artistique et technique, c'est un film parfait,' it commented. The following month it was released in France. 'Carol Reed, son auteur, s'affirme definitivement comme le plus brillant des realisateurs anglais et l'un des tout premiers du monde,' wrote André Bazin in *le Parisien libéré*.[5] Reed and Korda popped over to Paris for the French premiere, and on the same day were presented with their Cannes award, in the presence of the Cannes jury, by the French foreign minister Robert Schuman. Afterwards there was a reception at the Ritz, hosted – but certainly not paid for – by Orson Welles.[6]

Back in England *The Third Man* went on general release on 3 October in the same week as Laurence Olivier's *Hamlet*, which had recently won the Oscar for Best Film. In an age where films routinely appeared in the suburbs and provinces for a few days only and then were gone to make way for the next release, this was the cause of some annoyance. 'Fans will either have to miss one of these big attractions or go to the cinema twice in a week,' commented Reg Whiteley of the *Daily Mirror*.[7] 'Don't the film moguls realize that money is tough and that most people can't afford two visits to the locals in seven days?'

In the event *The Third Man* refused to go away. Many suburban and provincial cinemas rebooked it twice and sometimes three times. Meanwhile it continued on an unequalled West End run, after five weeks transferring from the Plaza, Piccadilly, to the Carlton, Haymarket, where – in spite of the fact that the film was by now showing all over the country – business increased with each successive week. After a two-week Christmas season at the Rialto, Coventry Street, it transferred back to the Plaza.

It wasn't until after Hogmanay that the film finally reached Scotland. It opened on Twelfth Night in the Regal Cinema, Edinburgh, with a special midnight showing. Such was the excitement that had already been generated by the film south of the border, and Karas's zither music – which was everywhere – that queues gathered outside the cinema in a freezing Scottish winter over three hours before the screening began.[8] As the credits began, the audience hummed along to the opening bars of music.

The only place where *The Third Man* received any seriously adverse criticism was – perhaps not surprisingly – Vienna. The Austrian Tourist Commission – an organisation which was then almost a contradiction in terms – was worried because the film perpetuated the image it was trying to discourage of Vienna as a dangerous place. On 10 March 1950 the Communist evening paper *Der Abend* denounced *The Third Man* on its front page for defaming the city as a 'robber's den' and described it as the work of 'modern gangsters'. Graham Greene was attacked as an author 'notorious for his utter trash', who in collaboration with Carol Reed 'went wild at the expense of this defenceless city'. The article also took issue with the unsympathetic depiction of the Soviets: 'Naturally the poison of Russian hatred is essential in such a cocktail. Thus a beautiful girl has had to fly to Czechoslovakia for some quite unknown reason. But it suffices that she is wanted by the Russians.'

In more measured tones the socialist *Arbeiter Zeitung* commented that 'some of the scenes are far from reality to a Vienna audience ... but what does a little inconsistency in the script matter if the sum total is such a sweeping success?' The *Neues Osterreich* took the film's achievement for granted, but urged its readers to spare a thought for the unsung heroes – the Viennese men and women who stood in for the stars. Orson Welles, it pointed out, only condescended to enter the sewers once he had been assured that they had been thoroughly disinfected and then 'he appeared in a cloud of perfume' (although even this seems to have overstated his Viennese involvement). The real Man of the Hour, the paper declared, was Welles' stand-in, a certain Viennese butcher called Otto Schusser, who did all the hard work sliding down heaps of rubble and running away.

While the Communists in Vienna dismissed the film as Western propaganda, Selznick worried that the 'very funny lines read by Welles at Ferris wheel about contrast with Switzerland might be considered Communist propaganda'.[9] He advised Korda to cut out the speech in some of the more sensitive European countries. 'Certainly under no circumstances should these lines be in picture when released in Switzerland.' He was particularly concerned because he didn't want to be party to anything that might undermine his strong anti-Communist reputation.

The film opened in America on 2 February 1950. There was a celebrity premiere at the Victoria Theater on Broadway, in aid of a charity for the blind. The guests, who included Joseph Cotten and several other Hollywood stars, arrived to the tune of 'The Harry Lime Theme', played over and over again by one of the legion of Karas impersonators who had sprung up since the film had first opened in London five months earlier.

The next day the New York papers gave their verdict. 'Probably American filmgoers' best of 1950,' commented *Time*. 'The work of a craftsman so skilled that he has earned the right to be judged as an artist.' The *New York Daily Mirror* called it, 'A complete, striking demonstration of the use of art for art's sake, with cinema moulds shattered effortlessly. Carol Reed is a picture Titan of genius.' The litany of praise was so insistent that Reed could probably have turned to the few more contrary responses with a sense almost of relief. The reviewer of the *New Yorker* was quite understandably fed up with zither music, which it was impossible get away from even if you hadn't seen the film – 'a little zither music goes a mighty long way with me, I find'. He thought that Reed had indulged 'entirely too much in trick camera angles to nudge along laggard episodes'. And in a cold and wintry New York he found Vienna's sewers 'probably the most sanitary in appearance of any in the world', more hospitable than menacing. 'I was inclined to think they might be a pleasant place to spend a hot afternoon.'

When the film opened soon afterwards on the West coast, Selznick's fears about Communist propaganda turned out not to be so far-fetched – at least as far as America was concerned. A Mr Dudley Steele of the Acme Sash Balance Company, Long Beach, wrote in to complain:

> Orson Welles has long been known to have certain decided leftish thinking. I am purposely being restrained in my statements concerning Mr Welles.
>
> All through the picture, after I had noted that Mr Welles had a part therein, I waited for what I was sure would inevitably follow, namely, some propoganda [sic] slanted along Communist lines. It was towards the last of the picture that Mr Welles stated something about Italy having produced the Renaissance . . . Immediately following these words he said with a sneer, 'Switzerland has been a Democracy for 500 years. What has it produced? The Cuckoo Clock.'
>
> The man is a master of facial and vocal inflection and his method of expressing what Switzerland had been and had produced was highly derogatory to democracy.
>
> Other than the above offensive language, it seemed to me the picture was excellent and I sincerely hope that you will eliminate the language just quoted. It does the picture no good.[10]

The tributes to *The Third Man* would scarcely diminish with the passing years. But perhaps the true measure of its importance is that just as many have been from film-makers as critics. '*The Third Man* [is] the only movie of mine I ever watch on television because I like it so much,' Orson Welles himself would comment. When Martin Scorsese was fourteen, his favourite Orson Welles performance was Harry Lime. He liked the movie so much that he went on to write a treatise on it at film school.* Recent allusions to the film have included Peter Jackson's *Heavenly Creatures* (1994) – with a pre-*Titanic* Kate Winslet fantasising over Harry Lime – and Mike Figgis's *Leaving Las Vegas* (1995) – Nick Cage as a Hollywood scriptwriter taking Holly Martins' self-loathing to its logical conclusion by drinking himself to death.†

---

* Although his tutor didn't share his taste. Awarding him a B+, he commented, 'Forget this, it's just a thriller.'
† Trying to keep track of all the allusions is a futile exercise. Yesterday (15 June 1999) I returned the corrected proofs of this book to my editor. I spent my first free evening in weeks in front of the television and watched the BBC drama *Silent Witness*. It began with a fire in a cinema. The film the audience had been watching was *The Third Man*: as the projection room burns, we see Alida Valli on the screen go up in flames. The plot of the episode concerned a crook who in Harry Lime fashion turns out not to have died when everyone thought he had died. Half a century later there is still no escape from *The Third Man*.

12

The Return of the Third Man

The Third Man's success led to a bandwagon of cash-ins. By public demand Lime cheated death yet again. In 1951 Orson Welles – who had originally made his name in radio – agreed to record a radio series called 'The Lives of Harry Lime'. It ran to 52 episodes. Each began with a pistol shot. Then, after a moment's silence, the laconic voice said: 'That was the shot that killed Harry Lime. He died in a sewer beneath Vienna. As those of you know who saw the movie *The Third Man*. Yes. That was the end of Harry Lime. But it was not the beginning. Harry Lime had many lives. And I can recount all of them. How do I know? It's very simple. Because my name is Harry Lime.'

It was an irresistible concept, its very premise contained in those opening disembodied lines of the film. 'I never knew the old Vienna before the war, with its Strauss music, its glamour and easy charm – Constantinople suited me better. I really got to know it in the classic period of the Black Market. We'd run anything, if people wanted it enough ...' Here was someone, who could have been Harry Lime, in *Sunset Boulevard* fashion, recalling an episode that ended with the death of Harry Lime.

But in the radio series Lime enjoyed a rehabilitation. The murderous racketeer became the beguiling rogue, dealing in an amiable cynicism. This was the kind of myth-making that once turned thieves and gunmen into the Wild West heroes that Holly Martins wrote about in his novels. Harry's charm was an indestructible thing.

The scriptwriters had fun building an earlier life for him.

His natural habitat was exotic *demi-monde* cities like Rio, Havana or Istanbul. On arrival, he'd head straight for the casino and, milling among the gaming tables in his tuxedo, soon find himself deep in an intrigue or a romance. Women, with names like Fifi, were always falling hopelessly in love with him. In '37 he had been running contraband out of Marseilles. Not long afterwards he was in Cairo on the run from the police of five different countries. Lime may have stayed in the best hotels, but right up to that last moment in the sewers of Vienna, as his fingers loosened their grasp on the grille that stood between him and freedom, he was a perpetual fugitive.

The transformation from the psychopathic criminal on Major Calloway's files into the suave confidence trickster of the radio series involved some compromises. Nonchalantly amoral, Harry was always up to one scam or another, but rarely with much success. At the last moment there would be a twist that would leave him empty-handed or with just a token prize – the reward money for a stolen jewel, but not the jewel itself. In his line of business, he would often explain to the listeners with wry detachment, you must expect to win some, lose some. Yet he made sure to lose in style, and if often he seemed not to have more than a few dollars to his name it didn't really matter because he could pay his bills with sheer charm.

There's a rough, on-the-hoof quality about these recordings. Listening to them, you find yourself doubting that Welles could have turned up for anything so troublesome as a rehearsal. Mostly it was pay-cheque work, like the sherry commercials he would undertake in later life. Yet as he rattles through the sort of lines that a bright twelve-year-old might write, you feel he's in his element. This, after all, was the man who described making movies as the biggest train-set a boy could hope to have.

Welles wrote a few episodes himself, and some were reprinted in a book called *The Lives of Harry Lime*, published in 1952 by the *News of the World*, where they had previously been serialised. One of the earliest, 'A Ticket to Tangier', was the fourth show to be broadcast on 24 August 1951. It's an excellent example of the new model Lime. Down on his luck in Paris, with only the price of a beer in his pocket, our hero reads a strange advertisement in a newspaper: 'Harry Lime will find a business opportunity of an extremely profitable nature in the city of Tangier.' There's no address or name or telephone number, but his eyes happen to wander a little further down the page to the personal column, where he reads this: 'Gentlemen travelling to Tangier – a visit to the desk of the porter at the Lancaster Hotel* on Rue de Berg will repay any business man planning a visit to Tangier who can whistle a certain tune.' Lime duly turns up at the hotel, doubtless whistling 'The Third Man Theme', and is given a manilla envelope with 50,000 francs and a ticket for Tangier.

On the aeroplane he flirts with a pretty air hostess, ringing the buzzer on his seat yet again towards the end of the flight. Perhaps in the early 1950s, when few people travelled abroad and the term 'jet set' had yet to be coined, the scene that followed would have had a freshness. But reading it now, it's hard to escape the echo of the countless films that have since made it a cliché:

> 'Yes, Mr Lime?'
>
> 'My name isn't Mr Lime,' I said. 'My name is Harry. Have you ever been to a night-club in Tangier called the Caballa?'
>
> 'Why, yes, I have,' she answered.
>
> 'Yes you have what?'
>
> She laughed. 'Yes, I have Harry.'
>
> 'Is it a nice night-club?' I asked.
>
> She replied that it was the best in town.
>
> 'That's good. I'm glad you like it. I've reserved a table there for us. OK?'
>
> There was a long pause. Then she said: 'Fasten your safety-belt. We're coming in.'
>
> Some hours later I remarked that she was one of

* As we have seen, Joseph Cotten's favourite hotel when he was staying in Paris.

the few girls outside of Havana who knew anything at
all about the rhumba.

'I learned it in Havana,' she said with a smile.

'That almost explains it.'

She asked me what I meant by 'almost'.

'I don't know. OK, you learned to dance in
Havana, but so do lots of other people. OK, you're a
hostess on an airline and you're very good-looking
and there are lots of good-looking hostesses that
dance the rhumba. But they don't dance that well,
and they're none of them that beautiful. No, I don't
know what I mean by almost – but really, you know,
you're almost too good to be true.'

'I'm not so good.'

'That's good.'

This is the repartee of a 60s spy movie; a dialogue which would
lend itself perfectly to the voice of Sean Connery. But in 1951,
when Welles wrote these lines James Bond had yet to be
thought of.

You can't help wondering whether Ian Fleming ever listened
to *The Lives of Harry Lime*, as he poured himself drinks on the
veranda of Goldeneye, his house in Jamaica. Maybe, it gave
him an inkling. A few months after 'A Ticket to Tangier' was
broadcast, in January 1952, he would start to write the first
Bond book, *Casino Royale* (Orson Welles appeared in the
movie version). Bond – international traveller, spy and anti-
hero, the man women couldn't resist – would in the years to
come conquer the best-seller lists and the movies, but he went
nowhere that Lime had not already been before.

If there's a distinctiveness about Welles' script contributions
it's that his Lime ultimately does have scruples. In 'A Ticket to
Tangier', the air hostess turns out to have set up the whole
trip. She's murdered her husband, a crook Harry Lime once
knew in Casablanca, and she wants Lime to help her dispose of
a cache of heroin. The situation has a teasing quality. Will he?
Won't he? Such is the moral ambivalence of Lime's character.
But by the end of the story Lime has tipped off the police

about the murder – 'You might call it the wages of Lime' – and worked out a scam with the heroin to enhance his new reputation as the resourceful and loveable rogue:

> I had no trouble in getting a good price in Marseilles the next week. But honestly, I don't approve of drugs. That's why I threw the original stuff into the Bay of Tangier and delivered several nicely wrapped packages of confectioner's sugar. So my conscience is clear.

It was an extraordinary about-turn for a character who in Vienna had shown no qualms about killing children with diluted penicillin. But the scriptwriters were not terribly consistent. Just a few weeks later, in the episode, 'Every Frame Has a Silver Lining', Harry Lime comes by fifty thousand dollars worth of opium in Tehran and tries to smuggle it back to America where it will fetch a good price.

But *The Lives of Harry Lime* was a happy-go-lucky venture and no one really cared about such inconsistencies. Part of the show's appeal for Welles must have been the opportunity it offered just to throw ideas around. It was the perfect testing ground. In one of the episodes Welles wrote, 'Man of Mystery', broadcast on 11 April 1952, Harry Lime tells the story of the mysterious Gregory Arkadian. It was a dry run for the film *Mr Arkadin* (*Confidential Report* in Britain) which Welles would make three years later.

There were also comic strips, and a 1959 TV spin-off starring Michael Rennie (although the producers had originally wanted James Mason), playing Harry Lime as an international art dealer cum amateur detective. Harry, the most depraved and evil of villains, was so beguiling that – just as Anna in the film cannot stop loving him – the film executives quickly turned him back into a hero too. 'From the sewers of Vienna to the television screens of today,' ran the BBC's selling slogan. The laid-back Harry, dressed in a sports jacket with a neatly pressed handkerchief in the top pocket – gone were the old coat and hat he wore in Vienna – frequented the world's sunniest beaches and most opulent night spots. His play-grounds would soon provide a familiar habitat for the gentlemen adventurers of countless 60s and 70s TV series. *The Saint, The Avengers, The Persuaders* – Harry was godfather to them all.

It wasn't until the 80s, the great decade of lost illusions, that anyone challenged the myth of Harry Lime. 'In fiction, he is tart but refreshing,' wrote David Thomson in his book *Suspects*. 'Whereas, in life, he was poison.'[1]

In this revisionist account, Lime was no longer the cool American, but a boy from Balham – English again, as Greene had originally conceived him. He was the only child of Constance Lime. Proprietress of a hairdressing salon, she worked hard to send her son to Dulwich. Here the young Lime got by 'cheating or stealing others' knowledge', and displayed an early talent for theatricals. After school he got a job as a car salesman, and became a wrestling impresario. During the Blitz he started up a salvage business and went into estate agency, buying up wrecked sites and reselling them. A feature of his business dealings was a readiness to profit out of the misery of others. When he set up the International Refugee Office, it seemed like a charitable gesture. He had the names of the well regarded on his letterhead, he visited America to champion the plight of refugees, but it was just a front. There is nothing admirable about this Harry at all, and somehow he departs even further from the original character than the whitewashes of the radio and TV series. Because the trouble with Harry is that we just can't help loving him, even when we know we shouldn't.

13

The Heart of the Matter

Graham Greene would take one of the biggest secrets of *The Third Man* to his grave. To unravel the mystery we must return to his trip to Vienna in that cold February of 1948. Although Elizabeth Montagu thought she was introducing Greene to Peter Smollett for the first time, possibly they had met before. During the war Smollett had worked for the Ministry of Information, where Greene in 1940 briefly held a post in the literature division. They also had an acquaintance in common, Kim Philby, who in 1963 would notoriously be exposed as a Soviet double-agent.

Greene met Philby for the first time in 1943, when he was posted to the Iberian department of the Secret Intelligence Service, which Philby ran. The two men became fast friends. In his memoir, *My Silent War,* Philby would recall their association at SIS as 'wholly delightful'. Greene 'added to the gaiety of the service'.[1]

Smollett's association with Philby went back much further. An Austrian national, his original name was Hans Peter Smolka, and he had met Philby in Vienna in 1934.

After the much earlier defections of the double-agents Burgess and Maclean, the newspapers took to dubbing Philby as 'the Third Man'. Greene in a newspaper article commented on the extraordinary coincidence that he should have created the expression before anyone could have applied it to his old boss. But the link between Harry Lime and Philby was more than just coincidence. The beginnings of *The Third Man* really lay in Philby's Vienna experiences a decade and a half before Greene himself visited the city.

Then Philby was an idealistic 22-year-old who had just graduated from Cambridge. He had come to Vienna to help support the socialist cause. The once proud capital of the Habsburg empire was now swollen with refugees from Hitler's Germany and subject to constant Nazi subversion. 'Red Vienna' had been in the control of the socialists since the end of the First World War, but an anti-socialist coalition had come to power in Austria by a narrow majority in 1932. A year later the Chancellor, Engelbert Dollfuss, dissolved parliament and began to rule by decree. As members of the recently crushed German Communist party fled into Austria, Vienna became the battleground for an increasingly bitter political struggle. With the freedom of movement that his British passport afforded, Philby made himself useful as a courier for an organisation called the Committee for Aiding Refugees from Fascism.

On 12 February 1934 the friction between Left and Right erupted into open civil war. For three days a battle raged between the socialist 'Schutzbund' on one side and the paramilitary Heimwehr and government forces on the other. Hundreds of people were killed. Dollfuss authorised the army to bombard the Karl Marx Hof, a huge complex of workers' tenements, which was a stronghold of the left-wing forces.

The Karl Marx Hof was considered to be the most enlightened and civilised example of public housing built anywhere. The howitzers which were turned on it dominated the headlines of the world, and served – in these days before the Spanish Civil War – as a powerful symbol of the struggle between Left and Right.

Philby joined the besieged socialists and helped many of them to escape into the sewers. One of his comrades was a young Communist called Litzi Friedmann – it was through her that he met Peter Smolka. With the suppression of the uprising on 15 February, Litzi may have feared arrest as the authorities tried to catch the ringleaders. In any event there was now clearly little hope for the Communist cause in Austria. So on 24 February Philby, who was already in love with Litzi, married her, giving her the protection of his passport. Two months later she obtained her own passport and the couple went to London.

In London Philby got a job as a sub-editor and helped to raise funds for Austrian communists. Now also in London was Peter Smolka. In late 1934 he set up a news agency, London Continental News, which gathered information from Central and Eastern Europe. Philby joined him in this venture, but it soon folded and the two went their separate ways.

Smolka changed his name to Smollett and continued his career in journalism. In 1938 he joined the Exchange Telegraph Agency, whose monitoring service of foreign broadcasts was a haven for left-wing refugees from fascism. He then wrote a series of favourable portraits of Soviet Russia for *The Times*, and later at the Ministry of Information became chief of the Soviet section.

Philby meanwhile was recruited by a Soviet agent in June of 1934; he buried his left-wing past, also pursued a career in journalism and eventually joined the Secret Intelligence Service. His wife Litzi knew about his work for Soviet intelligence and they agreed that they would have to separate in order not to compromise his newly acquired anti-Communist credentials. Litzi went to live in Paris in 1937. She returned to England when the war began, but she and Philby continued to live apart. They finally divorced in 1946 and Litzi went to live in East Berlin.

Anyone familiar with *The Third Man* will recognise the resemblances. In the original story – written by Greene after his visit to Vienna – Harry Lime works for the International Refugee Office, just as Philby worked for the Committee for Aiding Refugees from Fascism. In a tight spot both men find a means of escape through the city's sewers. Harry passes on information to the Russians, just as Philby does. Then there's Harry's girlfriend, Anna Schmidt; an illegal alien in Vienna, she fears arrest, just as back in 1934 – although for different

'I'm just a hack writer who drinks too much and falls in love with girls.' Graham Greene pours another one.

Below: His, alter ego, Holly Martins, confides in Major Calloway (Trevor Howard).

Joseph Cotten was in virtually every scene of *The Third Man*. Often grumpy and longing to get home, he must have envied his old friend – the much mentioned but rarely seen Orson Welles.

Orson Welles listening for a change. Carol Reed discusses the Big Wheel scene, while his assistant Guy Hamilton looks on.

The Third Man wasn't the first time that Joseph Cotten and Orson Welles had played two friends who fall out. Here in *Citizen Kane* Jed Leland watches a young Charles Foster Kane make a declaration of principles for his newspaper, the *Inquirer* – principles that he will one day betray.

Below: Holly Martins discovers that his old friend Harry Lime hasn't just lost his principles: he never had any in the first place.

The Third Man: Kim Philby entertaining reporters in 1955 after being cleared of tipping o
Burgess and Maclean. But his guests seem unconvinced.

Top Right: The Fourth Man: Anton Karas records the music, while Carol Reed, sitting on
sofa in the background, looks on.

Right: In Carol Reed's scrapbook of newspaper cuttings about the film, I came across this
pencil drawing. The words convey something of Reed's magnetic hold over not just zither
players but all his collaborators.

PORTRAIT OF A ZITHER PLAYER UNDER THE INFLUENCE OF SVENGALI REED

Sir Alexander Korda in his office at 146 Piccadilly. With characteristic elegance he worked at a bureau, not a desk. The French windows behind opened onto a small terraced garden, offering a view of Hyde Park in the distance. He seemed more like a distinguished Head of State than a film producer.

Alas, no such mistake could be made about David Selznick, Korda's partner and – just as often – adversary. The curtains are closed and the blinds are down. Producer through and through, he kept the real world firmly shut out of his office.

Third Man wins the Third Cannes Film Festival. Carol Reed admires his diploma.

The End.

reasons – Litzi Friedman feared arrest. Harry provides Anna with a forged passport, just as Philby, through marriage, provided Litzi with a British one. And Harry and Anna split up, just as Philby and Litzi do. In the film Anna would become a Czech, but in Greene's story she is a Hungarian. Litzi's father, who worked as a civil servant in Vienna, was of Hungarian Jewish origin.

The Third Man, both in fact and fiction, leads a double life. Kim Philby works for British intelligence, but spies for the Russians. Harry Lime pretends to run a medical charity, but is in fact in charge of a smuggling racket. But was this a conscious parallel? Did Graham Greene know that his friend was a spy years before he was forced to defect?

There were certainly grounds for suspicion. In 1942 Otto John, a German lawyer working for Lufthansa, made contact with British agents in Spain. Over the next two years he reported several initiatives by conspirators who wanted to overthrow Hitler and bring an early end to the war. Philby did all he could to suppress this information. In March 1944 Otto John met a British agent called Rita Winsor in Lisbon. He urged that the British support the Von Stauffenberg plot to kill Hitler, but Winsor told him that London had forbidden any further contact with representatives of the German opposition. After the plot's failure on 20 July 1944, John managed to escape to Madrid and then to Lisbon. He had planned to travel on to England, but was forced to stay in Portugal for several weeks, at considerable risk of being caught and killed by Gestapo agents. John would later recall: 'Rita Winsor confided to me that up to the very last moment someone in London had been resisting my entry into England – it was Philby.'[2] Greene, in charge of the Portugal desk, would have had a ringside view of his boss's extraordinary conduct. It would have been very difficult to understand – unless Philby had some commitment to the Soviet cause: the Russians feared an early peace that might leave Germany intact and threaten their ability to influence a post-war settlement.

Philby's conduct on the home front also gave Greene pause

for thought. By 1944 the Western allies had concluded that Germany could not win the war and that the long-term enemy was the Soviet Union. An anti-Soviet section was set up. Philby pushed to become its head, intriguing against a rival within the service. Greene realised that Philby wanted to involve him in this campaign of office politics, and resigned in May 1944. Writing of Philby in later years, Greene would explain that he 'resigned rather than accept the promotion which was a tiny cog in the machinery of his intrigue'.[3] This seems a trivial reason and, so soon before D-Day, it was an extraordinary time to opt for a comparatively dull job in the Political Intelligence Department of the Foreign Office. But Greene would only have had to ask himself why, of all sections, Philby should have been so keen to head Soviet counter-espionage for alarm bells to ring – especially after his boss's unusual behaviour in the case of Otto John. It's impossible to know for certain, but it seems likely that rather than betray his friend Greene chose to move on.

Peter 'Hans' Smolka also knew much more about Philby than he chose to let on. Gordon Brook-Shepherd, who as an officer in British military intelligence knew Smolka in Vienna after the war, remembered 'a fat rather unpleasant sinister-looking character'.[4] I found myself thinking of Sidney Greenstreet in *Casablanca* or *The Maltese Falcon*. 'He was a nasty piece of work ... We had no doubt at all that he was either a Soviet agent or working for both sides.'

The Soviets were suspicious of him too. In the summer of 1939 Smolka proposed that Philby should become a director at the Exchange Telegraph Agency, but Philby turned him down. In the mid-1980s, in the new era of *Glasnost*, he was able to describe his relationship with Smolka to the Russian writer Genrikh Borovik:

> I had met him back in Vienna. Whether he was a Communist or not, I do not know. He seemed to be, judging by his theoretical views – we had chatted

more than once. But from the point of view of his own lifestyle, his love of comfort, I would not consider him a Communist. From his totally unambiguous words, I knew that he might have accepted the change in my political mood and my departure from my left-wing friends, but he had no intention of believing it completely. He often demonstrated that by various hints. We used to run into each other at receptions and cocktail parties, and we had many friends in common. He often came to me with news items, and sometimes in the form of ordinary routine gossip he brought me very valuable information. And, you know, he would wink as he did it. He would tell me something truly important and wink – as if to say, You know what to do with this news. I got tired of that winking and I decided that we needed to rectify our equivocal relationship, otherwise it was in danger of going beyond the bounds of decency. He had become a naturalized citizen by then and held a rather significant position – head of the Russian section in the Ministry of Information.

So one time, I said to him, 'Listen, Hans, if in your present job you come across some information that in your opinion could help me in my work *for England*' – and I winked at him – 'come over to me and offer me two cigarettes. I'll take one, you'll keep the other, and that will be a signal that you want to tell me something important.'[5]

Philby's controllers in Moscow were furious that he had made such a proposal without their sanction and he was forced to break off relations with this particular informant. 'At the end of his story about Smolka,' recalled Borovik, 'Kim felt it necessary to stress one thing. Smolka knew a lot about him and about Burgess, and maybe he had known about the other members of the group. However, he had never told anyone about them ... In 1951 Guy Burgess and Donald Maclean defected to Moscow from London. Philby's name was mentioned in the press and Parliament; there were reasons for suspecting that he was the "third man". Smolka had to have known about it, but he did not turn him in even then."[6]

So when Graham Greene and Hans Smolka/Peter Smollett met in Vienna on 17 February 1948 – apparently for the first time – they had a lot to talk about. Their dinnertime meeting stretched into the early hours of the morning.[7] They were possibly the only two people west of the Iron Curtain who knew that Philby was a traitor. On the same day – six days after his arrival in Vienna, it is important to note, and a week before his departure – Greene would write to Catherine Walston 'the story is crystallising & I'm longing to get away'. Did the evening with Smolka and what he knew about Philby help to determine the shape of that story? The circumstances would seem to suggest it. But in his memoirs Greene gave a very different version:

> I had allowed myself not more than two weeks in
> Vienna before meeting a friend in Italy where I
> intended to write the story, but what story? There
> were three days left and I had no story, not even the
> storyteller, Colonel Calloway, whom I see now always
> in my mind with the features of Trevor Howard.
>   On the penultimate day I had the good fortune to
> lunch with a young British Intelligence officer (the
> future Duke of St Albans) – my wartime connection
> with the SIS used to bring me useful dividends in
> those days.[8]

According to Greene, the intelligence officer, Charles Beauclerk, gave him the background details to his story – the underground police and the sewers and the penicillin racket. But it's much more likely that Greene was using Beauclerk, then head of the British Information Office in Vienna, as a smokescreen. I can imagine Greene taking particular delight in that last sentence about the 'useful dividends' of SIS connections – it was an in-joke that only a very few people would have been able to share. Kim Philby perhaps chuckled over it in his *apparatchik* flat in Moscow. The more one becomes aware of the inconsistencies and deliberate untruths in Greene's various attempts at autobiography the more they seem like an elaborate game, in which he dished out generous helpings of fiction in the same way as his fiction so often gave a disguised version of his own life.

Back in 1948 there were very good reasons for keeping quiet about Smolka. Greene didn't want to give away any clues that might reveal the true inspiration for his story. *The Third Man* was really the ultimate coded message. Philby could have read in it his past, his present and what might so easily have been his future. When I talked to Gordon Brook-Shepherd, he expressed surprise that there was really nothing in the film about spying – because that was the one thing he remembered going on in Vienna all the time. But the last thing Greene must have wanted was for people to think of spies. That really would have given the game away. 'A person doesn't change because you find out more,' says Anna after Holly Martins has discovered that his friend is a murderer and a racketeer. In the event Greene would remain as loyal to Philby as Anna had to Harry.

In his last years Kim Philby began to make arrangements for his funeral. When asked what his great wish was, he is said to have replied: 'To have Graham Greene opposite me and a bottle of wine on a table between us.'[9] *Glasnost* made this wish come true – the two men met again in Moscow in 1986. Perhaps inevitably one wonders what past favours Philby might have wanted to express his gratitude for. Greene's silence perhaps – although it was too much to expect him to remain completely silent. Just being a writer meant he was bound to want to have his say somehow, even if it was in the secret code of *The Third Man*.

Greene and Philby met several times before Philby died in 1988. 'It was a most moving reunion,' commented Philby's Russian wife, 'between comrades who had served together in

World War Two. It was as if nothing had passed between them, there was much laughter and wine and good food. It went on for days.'[10] Three years later, in 1991, Greene died in the land of the cuckoo clocks, Switzerland – Harry Lime would have found that funny – and what exactly he knew about Philby remained un-revealed. He might have got into serious trouble if it had been otherwise. Imagine the headline: 'Knight of the Realm Harbours Traitor'. But perhaps maintaining such silence wasn't simply a matter of prudence, or a continued loyalty to Philby; perhaps too it was a loyalty to his writer's vocation. The plain truth – the unalloyed, unqualified truth, fact unmixed with fiction – enfeebles a writer, for then what is there left to wonder or say?

The Third Man wasn't the first time that Greene had mapped out something of Philby's life. He did the same more than ten years earlier in his novel *The Confidential Agent*, although then he had yet to meet Philby. D is an agent for the legitimate socialist government of a country embroiled in a civil war with rebel forces – it is never mentioned, but Spain is clearly the model. The agent is sent to Britain to negotiate a contract for vital supplies of coal. Agents from the opposing side attempt to scupper the deal. First they try to buy him out. Then, when they discover that he cannot be bought, they try to kill him. But D must also contend with his own side. His idealism is so little believed that they keep him under close surveillance. 'No amount of service would ever convince them that he hadn't got, at some level, a price. After all, he recognised sadly, *they* had their price: the people had been sold out over and over again by their leaders.' D discovers the loneliness of having principles.

When *The Confidential Agent* was published in 1939, Kim Philby had been in Spain for over two years during the Spanish Civil War. His Soviet controllers had wanted him to send back intelligence from the Franco side. Travelling there as a free-lance journalist, he later got a post with *The Times* and submitted pieces which were mostly sympathetic to the

Nationalists. To do so was to seem to disavow the Republican cause in which he passionately believed, and to earn the contempt of former left-wing friends. On 31 December 1937 during the battle for Teruel he survived a Republican shell which killed three other journalists. When General Franco gave him a medal for his miraculous escape, disapproving questions were asked in Parliament about his acceptance of the award. His former liberal and left-wing friends would have looked upon his conduct in Spain with disgust. Eric Gedye, a respected correspondent of the *Daily Telegraph*, whom Philby had known as a young man in Vienna, asked a mutual friend 'to tell him I was very sorry to find him in such bad company'.[11] Philby replied: 'Tell Eric not to be misled by appearances. I'm exactly what I've always been.'[12] This foolhardy compromise of his cover suggests the misery that his hidden loyalty must have occasioned. It required him to endure a loneliness every bit as deep as Greene's agent.

The notion of the Soviet Union as a champion of equality and justice became increasingly absurd during the 1930s, but Philby remained loyal to his Soviet masters 'in the confident faith that the principles of the Revolution would outlive the aberration of individuals, however enormous'. In his memoir he turned to his old wartime friend to explain this conduct: 'Graham Greene, in a book called *The Confidential Agent*, imagines a scene in which the heroine asks the hero if his leaders are any better than the others. "No, of course not," he replies. "But I still prefer the people they lead – even if they lead them all wrong ... You choose your side once and for all – of course it may be the wrong side. Only history can tell that." '[13]

You can't help wondering when Philby first read *The Confidential Agent*. Was it after he left Spain in August of 1939? The book would have been just out in the bookshops then. He might easily have bought a copy on the strength of the title alone. After all, a confidential agent was just what *he* was. The themes of idealism, treachery and loyalty that Greene's novel explored would have preoccupied him since he first became a spy for the Soviets back in 1934.

Was it really a coincidence that these two men should a few years later work together? They were such kindred spirits that perhaps they were always going to stumble into each other. Philby would have been drawn to the man who had explained his hidden life, just as Greene would have been drawn to the living embodiment of his novels – his word made flesh. It's impossible to know how many candidates the Head of the Iberian Section might have interviewed for the Portugal desk job, but once Greene walked in no one else would have stood a chance.

The idea of Kim Philby as the Third Man is enormously appealing, but it was not a literal correspondence. Greene simply took some of the circumstances of his friend's life to clothe a very different character. Kim Philby had strong ideals, even if they turned out to be the wrong ones; Harry Lime had none. The 'Third Man' was an amalgam, drawing as much on Greene's own imagination and life as on what he might have known about Philby. Again he was mixing fact and fiction.

As a writer Greene had few scruples about repeating himself. The same characters, with variations, pop up again and again in his work. You can find a primitive version of Harry Lime as long ago as Greene's 1932 novel *Stamboul Train*. The Viennese thief Josef Grünlich seduces Anna, a stationmaster's wife, so that he can gain access to her husband's safe. When the husband makes an unexpected entrance, Grünlich murders him and escapes on the Orient Express. So far from feeling any guilt, he revels in his new status as a murderer and prides himself on his criminal skills. Ten years later, in *The Ministry of Fear*, this psychopath had evolved into the sophisticated Nazi spy Willi Hilfe, who has a philosophy of evil. Of all Greene's novels, *The Ministry of Fear*, set in a blitzed London, most closely resembles *The Third Man* with its equally war-torn setting.

Arthur Rowe wins a cake at a fete, and is nearly killed when a stranger tries to get the cake back. Determined to get to the bottom of this mystery, he visits the Free Mothers, the charity which organised the fair. Here he enlists the help of two of the charity workers, Willi and Anna Hilfe. Brother and sister, they are both refugees from Vienna.

After Rowe has told his extraordinary story about the stranger prepared to murder him for a cake, the conversation takes an easy turn to the state of the war-torn world. 'There's no longer a thing called a criminal class,' comments Hilfe. 'There were lots of people in Austria you'd have said couldn't ... well, do the things we saw them do ... in these days it really pays to murder, and when a thing pays it becomes respectable. The rich abortionist becomes a gynaecologist and the rich thief a bank director.'

As Greene describes Rowe's shock 'at being told by a young man of great experience that there was no division between the worlds', the words of another cynic come to mind: 'Nobody thinks in terms of human beings,' Harry Lime tells Holly Martins. 'Governments don't, so why should we? They talk about the people and the proletariat, I talk about the suckers and the mugs. It's the same thing.'

It's not much of a surprise when Hilfe turns out to be a Nazi agent who's after a roll of microfilm which had been concealed in the cake. With his 'charm and ease' and 'his amusing nihilistic abandon' he's a twin soul of Harry Lime, shrugging off evil with the same sort of laugh. He can grin as he explains the 'tragic necessity' of a failed attempt to kill his own sister. 'He seemed to accuse them of a lack of humour; it was not the kind of thing they ought to have taken to heart.' And even when he knows the game is up, he still retains an 'air of badinage'.

Arthur Rowe finally corners Hilfe in a Gents in Paddington Railway Station, where he meets his end just a length of plumbing away from the sewers in which Harry meets his:

> The stone floor was wet and he slipped but recovered.
> He began to pull at a lavatory door, but of course it

was locked. He didn't seem to know what to do: it
was as if he needed to get behind a door, out of
sight, into some burrow ... He turned and said
imploringly, 'Give me a penny' ... Hilfe's strained
white face begged for his pity. Pity again. [Rowe] held
out a penny to him and then tossed it and walked up
the steps; before he reached the top he heard the
shot. He didn't go back: he left him for others to
find.

Rowe helps to put a beast out of its misery. In *The Third Man*,
Holly Martins himself administers the *coup de grâce*:

[He] crawled up the passage to the foot of the iron
stairs. Thirty feet above his head was the manhole,
but he wouldn't have had the strength to lift it, and
even if he had succeeded the police were waiting
above. He must have known all that, but he was in
great pain, and just as an animal creeps into the dark
to die, so I suppose a man makes for the light. He
wants to die at home, and the darkness is never
home to *us*. He began to pull himself up the stairs,
but then the pain took him and he couldn't go on.
For a moment I thought he was dead, but then he
whimpered with pain. I said 'Harry,' and he swivelled
his eyes with great effort to my face. He was trying to
speak, and I bent down to listen. 'Bloody fool,' he
said – that was all ... Then he began to whimper
again. I couldn't bear it any more and I put a bullet
through him.

Arthur Rowe is as 'determined to get to the bottom of
things' as Holly Martins, and he also falls in love with a girl
called Anna. At first, 'happily drunk with danger and action',
he imagines that everything is simple. 'He was helping in a
great struggle, and when he saw Anna again he could claim to
have played a part against her enemies...' But as his
investigation progresses, he learns 'the lesson most people
learn very young, that things never work out in the expected

way. This wasn't an exciting adventure, and he wasn't a hero.' In *The Third Man* Major Calloway says something rather similar when he tells Holly Martins not to interfere with the police's investigations: 'This isn't Santa Fe, I'm not a sheriff, and you aren't a cowboy . . .'

When Greene revised *The Ministry of Fear* after the war, he added, in ironic counterpoint to the narrative, epigraphs taken from Charlotte M. Yonge's historical romance *The Little Duke*. It was one of Greene's favourite books when he was a child. But the adult writer realises that 'the Little Duke is dead and betrayed and forgotten; we cannot recognize the villain and we suspect the hero and the world is a small cramped place'. The heroes in the Westerns Holly Martins writes may have names like the Oklahoma Kid or the Lone Rider of Santa Fe, but they are just frontier versions of Charlotte M. Yonge's 'Little Duke'.

The Third Man begins where the previous Greene–Reed collaboration left off. Holly Martins resembles the little boy in *The Fallen Idol* – he misunderstands the behaviour of the grown-ups, he confuses fact with fiction. The film traces the stages in his getting of wisdom. When finally he discovers the truth about Harry, he realises that the rules of his Westerns do not apply to life's complexities. There's no place for the Oklahoma Kid in the Vienna of 1949. 'I suppose he was laughing at fools like us all the time,' he says bitterly of his old friend, and he decides to leave the investigation to the police. 'I'm leaving Vienna. I don't care whether Harry was murdered by Kurtz or Popescu – or the third man. Whoever killed him, there was some sort of justice. Maybe I would have killed him myself.' It's a moment of profound disillusionment. Rowe experiences a similar moment in *The Ministry of Fear* when he learns that Hilfe – the brother of the woman he loves – is a Nazi spy: 'Rowe realized that if he wished he could telephone to Mr Prentice and have the police surround the flat – he was no longer anxious for glory; the sense of adventure had leaked away and left only the sense of human pain.'

*

Anna, or Anne, was a favourite name for Greene's heroines. Anna Schmidt in *The Third Man* was really the latest version of a character that can be traced back to Anne Crowder in Greene's 1936 novel *A Gun for Sale*. Like Anna Schmidt in *The Third Man*, this Anne is an actress. The description of the dowdy pantomime she appears in has much of the same atmosphere as the down-at-heel Viennese theatre shown in the film.

Anne befriends the political assassin Raven, and becomes the first person in his life that he feels able to trust. But she has an ulterior motive: she wants him to lead her to his paymasters so that a war can be averted. Her pursuit of this higher ideal leads her to betray Raven in the end. The varieties of loyalty and the conflicts of principle that they entailed were Greene's consuming interest. In *The Ministry of Fear* Anna Hilfe reveals her brother's treachery, but gives him the chance to escape.

The Anna of *The Third Man* was Greene's most uncompromising. Anna Schmidt's loyalty to Harry Lime is total. Even once she has discovered that he is a murderer and has betrayed her to the Russians, it does not change. She refuses to cooperate with the police and has only contempt for Holly Martins' decision to do so. When the police lie in wait for Harry Lime to meet Holly in a café it is Anna who warns him away. She plays no part in his final entrapment.

The extraordinary thing is the difference between the original story and the final film, which, as Greene himself pointed out, is 'better than the story because it is in this case the finished state of the story'. In the story Anna watches her lover being buried and then walks off with the man who shot him. Calloway, who provides the narrative voice, describes Martins 'striding off on his overgrown legs after the girl. He caught her up and they walked side by side. I don't think he said a word to her: it was like the end of a story except that before they turned out of my sight her hand was through his arm – which is how a story usually begins.'

If Greene really held the view that 'an entertainment of this kind was too light an affair to carry the weight of an unhappy ending',[14] then Carol Reed – or David Selznick – 'triumphantly right', protected him from himself. With her implacable character, Anna was the embodiment of that most rare and prized commodity at the heart of all Greene's novels, trust. He wrote about it as if it were as integral a part of society as the atoms that made up matter, the universal principle into which all human relations could be resolved. He wrote about it with all the feverish obsessiveness of someone who had been badly betrayed himself.

14

The Little Duke

'There was a deep scar long after the pain had ceased.'
Charlotte M. Yonge, *The Little Duke*

At the age of thirteen, after a sheltered and happy childhood, Graham Greene was sent to St John's, a boarding house at Berkhamstead School, where his father was headmaster. He was bookish, useless at games and had a funny voice. He was teased mercilessly. He had no one to turn to. If he sought the help of his father, as another boy might have done, he would be accused of treachery. His unhappiness led to attempts at self-mutilation and suicide. Finally at sixteen he ran away. 'I endured that life for some eight terms,' he wrote in his memoir *A Sort of a Life*, 'a hundred and four weeks of monotony, humiliation and mental pain.'[1]

Chief among his tormentors were two boys called Carter and Wheeler. 'Carter had an adult imagination – he could conceive the conflict of loyalties, loyalties to my age-group, loyalty to my father and brother. The sneering nicknames were inserted like splinters under the nails.'[2] For Carter, Greene felt a grudging admiration of the kind that often exists between the tortured and their torturers, but Wheeler's crime was unforgivable because once he had been a friend. 'With his defection my isolation had become almost complete.'[3]

The disillusionments of youth harden into a permanent impression of the world, which subsequent experience may mollify but never completely efface. The torment Greene had endured at school would replay itself endlessly in his writing.

Few other writers can rival his collection of damaged, scarred or hunted people. All, to some degree, seem like versions of himself.

There's Raven, the assassin of *Gun for Sale*, who trusts nobody. 'People don't trouble to keep their word to me,' he says. 'If a man's born ugly, he doesn't stand a chance. It begins at school.' Here's the experience of a bullied boy who knew how people could pick on a weakness. Raven had a hair-lip; the young Greene lisped, he couldn't march straight in school parades, couldn't hold his catches in cricket matches. In the same novel, the police detective Saunders has a stammer. When he's asleep, he dreams of being free of his speech impediment. Greene was drawn to such afflictions with the fascination and sympathy of a fellow sufferer.

Holly Martins in *The Third Man* was just the latest in a long roll call of inadequates. In a moment of self-pity he describes himself as 'a hack writer who drinks too much and falls in love with girls'. Of all Greene's alter egos, he seems the most thinly disguised. He goes to the same city, drinks in the same bars. And just like Raven, it began at school. Harry Lime, he confides to Major Calloway, was his only friend at school. 'I was never so lonesome in my life until he showed up.' The fact that he thinks of Lime as 'the best friend I ever had' only makes him seem a more pathetic figure. He may show his own loyalty by doing what he can to clear his friend's name, but in return Harry sends his henchmen after him when he learns too much.

The Third Man was the formulation of a question that Greene asked with an almost pathological insistence: Will someone who professes to be a friend remain true? It can be traced back through all the fictional betrayals of the novels to Wheeler the school friend whose defection caused such misery. This was the Original Sin in Greene's mental landscape, the cause of a trauma that meant he would greet every betrayal, however 'justified' it might seem, with consternation. Once Holly Martins has discovered that Lime is an evil racketeer, he helps the police to catch him. It's the 'right' thing to do, but he seems diminished for having done so. We understand perfectly as Anna walks past him without even a single glance. In *A Gun for Sale* Anne Crowder's betrayal of Raven stops a war. She can look forward to a nation's gratitude for her part in the 'sensation of the century', but it makes no difference to her conscience: ' "All the same," Anne said, as Raven covered her with his sack: Raven touched her icy hand, "I failed." '

In *The Third Man* Anna will not help the police to catch Lime even though he has betrayed her. Her loyalty, so defiant of human reason, evokes a kind of appalled admiration. There's a touch of a Philby committing himself once and for all to Communism in spite of its manifest flaws. In an introduction to Philby's memoirs, Greene would write: 'Like many Catholics who, in the reign of Elizabeth, worked for the victory of Spain, Philby has a chilling certainty in the correctness of his judgement, the logical fanaticism of a man who, having once found a faith, is not going to lose it because of the injustices or cruelties inflicted by erring human instruments.'

Greene was attracted to such people. Their fixed natures answered to his own need for security. The bullied boy turns in on himself, fears confiding in people who will abuse his trust, but at the same time, in his self-created solitude, craves such confidences with twice the longing.

As a young man at Oxford, Greene had a tendency to form deep but ultimately fruitless romantic attachments. Objects of his affection included his sister's governess, a cousin and a waitress in Oxford called Rose – another name which would work its way more than once into his fiction. However short-lived these relationships may have been, they weren't light undergraduate affairs but matters of the heart. He was looking to love without reserve. The waitress called him 'soft'.

In his last year at Oxford, Greene published an article about sex, religion and the cinema in which he wrote, 'We either go to Church and worship the Virgin Mary or to a public house and snigger over stories and limericks.'[4] Vivien Dayrell-Browning, a nineteen-year-old girl who had converted to

Catholicism, wrote back to correct him on his terminology. One did not 'worship' the Virgin Mary, she pointed out, one 'venerated' her, the correct term being 'hyperdulia'. Greene invited Vivien to tea and duly proceeded to venerate her.

The next two years were a hyperdulia of endless flowers, letters and entreaties. Vivien was fond of him but distant, and his proposals of marriage were repeatedly turned down. But where others might have soon given up hope, or switched their affections to an easier challenge, Greene persevered relentlessly. He was the Little Duke battling bravely for his lady's hand. There was a sort of forlorn chivalry, which Holly Martins' futile courtship of Anna and his Quixotic attempts to clear a dead friend's name resembled.

A major stumbling block in Greene's eventually more successful courtship was his lack of religious belief. He finally converted to Catholicism in order to marry Vivien, but the extraordinary determination with which he wooed her leaves the impression of someone who would in any case have found in the Roman Catholic Church a natural home. What drew him to her in the first place was the certainty of belief that Catholicism could offer.

I can remember from my own childhood the intensity of a religion where everything encouraged devotion. I was startled recently to discover that Graham Greene had got married in the church where I had been an altar boy – St Mary's, in Holly Place, Hampstead. Greene would have liked the names of our two priests – Father Morrell (pronounced 'Moral') and Father Body. Probably not much had changed between his wedding day in 1927 and my arrival there as a ten-year-old well over forty years later. He would have looked upon the same large canvas above the high altar depicting the Assumption of the Virgin Mary, and, along the walls of the church, the same fourteen Stations of the Cross.

A High Mass was some display, the officiating priest attended by a Master of Ceremonies, a Cross-bearer, two torch-bearers, two acolytes and a thurifer. During the Eucharist, everything would slip into another dimension as the congregation knelt, and the priest turned the bread and wine into the Body and Blood of Christ. The church was smoky with incense, the congregation fading into soft focus, briefly insubstantial in this quietest moment. Greene would have liked the way the Catholic Church was so much bigger than any individual: he had to lose himself in something beyond the determination of fickle humans, whether it was love, alcohol or prayer.

Recently I returned to Holly Place. I don't know if this story is true, but I remember being told that the church was built at a time when Catholics were still persecuted in this country. Architecturally plain and sandwiched between two town houses, it was designed to be easily concealed. Were it not for a short, squat bell tower, you'd never know that there was even a church there. It seemed appropriate that the persecuted and secretive Greene should have been married in such a place.

As I listened to the Gospel reading, from Matthew 19, I couldn't help but think how Anna would have approved. The Pharisees ask Jesus whether it is ever lawful for a man to divorce his wife:

> He asked in return, 'Have you never read that the creator made them from the beginning male and female?'; and he added, 'For this reason a man shall leave his father and mother, and be made one with his wife; and the two shall become one flesh. What God has joined together, man must not separate.' 'Why then', they objected, 'did Moses lay it down that a man might divorce his wife by note of dismissal?' He answered, 'It was because your minds were closed that Moses gave you permission to divorce your wives; but it was not like that when all began.'

When Anna hears of Harry's death, her life loses all meaning. 'I don't know anything any more except I want to be dead too,' she tells Holly Martins. Having committed herself to Harry, nothing on earth will break her trust.

But Anna represented just one pole in Greene's nature. He longed for trust, yet just as often broke it. In later years his neglect of Vivien would be as concentrated as his original pursuit of her had been. She was either the Adored Wife or the Abandoned Wife. There was no in between. The notion of betrayal, which he so endlessly pondered, exerted a kind of masochistic pull: he was fascinated and intrigued by it, as at school he had felt a reluctant admiration for his tormentor, Carter.

Perhaps the whole bullied boy's experience meant that just as he had longed to pledge his heart he was as likely to snatch it away again. Certainly it would have bred a contempt as easily as a longing to love. It's hard to be generous to your fellow-men when they have tripped you up and taken pleasure in your embarrassment. If the character Anna expressed Greene's longing for trust, then Harry Lime grew out of his fear that there wasn't any. In such a world, where 'nobody thinks in terms of human beings', you resort to unbridled egoism. No pun on Greene's full name (Henry Graham Greene) was needed to suggest the appeal that Harry Lime might also have held for Greene.

For someone so preoccupied by man's contradictory nature, the Catholic Church with its rich symbolism provided an ideal framework. With its confessional offering redemption, no other religion embraced the saints and the sinners so completely. Scarred by the disappointments that he had suffered and obsessed by the conflicts of competing loyalties, he would have been attracted by both the commitment that Catholicism expected and the certainty that it could provide. It was some solace perhaps as he struggled to come to terms with the several selves that warred in the aftermath of the Little Duke's betrayal.

15

The Storyteller

When the stories of *The Third Man* and *The Fallen Idol* were published together, Graham Greene wrote in the preface: 'Of one thing about both these films I have complete certainty, that their success is due to Carol Reed, the only director I know with that particular warmth of human sympathy, the extraordinary feeling for the right face for the right part, the exactitude of cutting, and not least the power of sympathising with an author's worries and an ability to guide him.'

For all the quarrels that took place between Korda and Selznick, *The Third Man* was in the end a monument to a perfect collaboration. Greene had found somebody he could trust at last. Reed was perhaps the ideal director to get the best out of him. Famously adept at dealing with children and animals, it was not surprising that he should also have had a way with the bullied – one recalls him taking Guy Hamilton to task for making fun of the afflicted people he found in Vienna's soup kitchens.

Hamilton remembered the two of them together in Vienna before filming began. A favourite haunt was the Oriental. 'The tattiest, the most terrible nightclub of all nightclubs . . . It was dark and damp, and there were these totally talentless strippers, from Russia, from Czechoslovakia, they were very sad ladies, and Carol said marvellous! We've got to shoot in here and I think we did. And Graham was there getting solemnly pissed, and it was the first Graham Greene line that ever hit me. He said, "Don't you sense evil?" '[1]

Greene was fascinated by this club as a hellish place, but

Reed was drawn to the individuals, not judging but attentive to the dramas of people caught in difficult circumstances. There was something pitiless about Greene's view. Reed softened it. His humanity balanced out Greene's inclination to look for people's weaknesses. 'I mean if there was sin going around,' recalled Guy Hamilton, 'if you said to Graham, tonight, at three o'clock in the morning, I can take you to a central place, he'd be off. There was a sort of necessity of dividing sin and sinners, which was not Carol's scene at all.' While Greene drew on his own suffering and experience, Reed was the fascinated observer. The detached, sardonic quality of *The Third Man* seems to me to owe much more to Reed than it does to Greene. The brilliance of his best work lay not in putting forward a point of view, but in an intuitive feel for the way people are and what they do.

Elizabeth Montagu was intrigued by their attitude to each other. 'Sometimes you had the feeling that they were tremendously together. Other times you felt they were watching each other like two cats.' Of the two, Montagu felt Carol Reed was 'by far the stronger character'.

Part of that strength revealed itself in the lack of creative egotism with which he worked with Greene. He did not seek to make *The Third Man* his own, but sought faithfully to interpret Greene's conception. The film world, peopled with more than its fair share of Carters and Wheelers, was about the last place Greene could have hoped to find such creative loyalty.

For Reed a career in the cinema must have seemed an entirely natural step to take. Son of the celebrated actor-manager Sir Herbert Beerbohm Tree, he attended the Italia Conti stage school as a child and was briefly an actor before becoming a personal assistant to Edgar Wallace in 1926.

Wallace could knock out best-selling thrillers and adventure stories in an unending stream. He had switched successfully to plays and, when Reed joined him, had just started on a venture to turn them into films. Perhaps the defining feature of these early years was the phenomenal industry that Reed's work for Wallace involved. Wallace often had as many as three plays running in London at the same time. Reed might act in one, supervise the second, and direct the third. This apprenticeship would have encouraged a down-to-earth professionalism.

The partnership came to an end when Wallace died out in Hollywood, where he had just finished working on the script of *King Kong*. One mentor was soon replaced by another, when the film producer Basil Dean, who had worked with Reed's father, and had made his first films at Edgar Wallace's Beaconsfield studios, offered him a job as a dialogue coach and assistant director for his Associated Talking Pictures at Ealing.

Dean's reputation for autocratic harshness was legendary. A typical Dean anecdote tells of the guardian angel who spotted a man about to commit suicide. The angel intervenes, but when the man explains tearfully that he works for Basil Dean the angel starts to cry too. But Reed still managed to make himself indispensable, winning Dean's admiration and approval.

Dean was an unusual mixture of the theatrical and the filmic. While he was in charge of Ealing, he continued to produce plays on the West End stage, and many of his films at Ealing were adaptations of theatrical productions. Yet he went to lengths to invest these films with realism, often shooting on location at a time when this was difficult to do and insisting on authentic detail. Graham Greene, who once wrote a film for Dean, recalled how he held up production for an afternoon until the right kind of sugar could be found to put in the actors' coffee during a dinner party scene. Rather than employ screenwriters, Dean preferred to work with established playwrights or novelists. Gracie Fields musicals and George Formby comedies may have been the commercial mainstay of the Ealing studios in the 1930s, but Dean employed such distinguished dramatists as J.B. Priestley and Walter Greenwood to write them.

In a way *The Third Man* was the finest achievement of the Basil Dean school of film-making. Close collaboration with an established author, location shooting, an emphasis on actors' performances – these were all things that Reed's training at Associated Talking Pictures would have encouraged. The crucial difference was that Reed possessed a touch of genuine inspiration to add to Dean's dogged belief in quality.

Dean's own films are characterised by a rather dour literalism; but Reed's realist approach was entwined with a lyricism and a sense of the fantastic. The everyday coexisted with the magical. He had a conjuror's feel for making things appear and disappear with style – there was no puff of smoke when Harry Lime appeared in the doorway but it was a genie's entrance.

It was a mark of the kind of professional film-maker Reed was that he always thought very carefully about how an audience would respond to a scene. As Guy Hamilton recalled, the charladies at Shepperton Studios were an important part of the film-making effort:

> There used to be two old charladies charging around, sweeping around the cutting rooms and what have you. And whenever there was a point of discussion, [Carol would] hold everything and send for the charladies. I mean I'll pick an imaginary scene. The villain says, 'Charles, how about a whisky? Say when.' It's poison that's being poured in, and the bottle's got POISON written large ... Carol says I bet you they don't notice. And everybody was saying, 'Carol, don't be fucking silly, it's got POISON written and he's doing that.' And he says, 'Hold everything. Send for the charladies.' And so these two darling charladies come in. And they're quite used to it, these two. 'Oh, hello, Carol.' 'Now you'll see in this scene two gentlemen. They're talking. The one in the evening dress doesn't like the other one very much. That's all you need to know. Right, run the scene.'[2]

If as usual Reed was right, the charladies wouldn't notice the word 'poison' on the bottle and some other way would have to be thought of to convey the protagonist's intention. The aim was 'total clarity in storytelling, so that you don't have to be the brains of Britain to follow the scene'.

These sessions were the more human equivalent of the Hollywood preview. While Selznick sought the advice of the paying customers, Reed turned to the people he knew and worked with. In the case of *The Third Man*, recalled Noreen Best, he was 'very worried about the last shot of the film' – Valli walking down the cemetery path. 'He held that shot for so long, which was very unusual, and he had us all in separately to watch it and to see if it would hold.'

'Carol was a storyteller,' observed Hamilton, 'and he passed that on to me. Your function is to tell stories. He believed that direction was the second oldest profession in the business. After prostitution there was the storyteller in the square in Bethlehem or Baghdad or wherever it is. "Gather round, people, I will tell you a story." And if you told the story well, they filled your bowl and you ate well. If you told the story badly, they all pissed off, and you'd better get an honest job. I mean that was his fundamental belief.'

The film-makers Reed admired most were the great directors of classical Hollywood cinema. He used to talk a lot about John Ford. He was envious of his control over pacing – the way he could have Wayne come out of a saloon, walk over to his horse, climb on, and still hold an audience's attention. He felt – I think wrongly – that if he had tried the same thing, he wouldn't have got away with it. But his respect for Ford was widely shared in the school of directing to which he belonged. Howard Hawks once commented: 'A very good man, asked to name the three best directors, said John Ford, John Ford, John Ford. And most of us who have studied that kind of thing, we agree on that.'[3]

Reed got his first chance to direct in 1935 with the children's adventure story *Midshipman Easy*. 'It did not occur to me to wonder if the script was good or bad. I accepted it with gratitude,'[4] he commented. It was an attitude which contrasted notably with his contemporary, David Lean. In the thirties Lean enjoyed the reputation as the best editor in British features. For years people had been trying to persuade him to direct, but he held out until he could do so on a big budget prestige picture.

After *Midshipman Easy*, Reed made *Laburnum Grove* and several more routine assignments. He didn't look down on this material, but breathed life into it. Two-dimensional characters became plausible on the screen. A few critics spotted a promising talent. One of the first was Reed's future collaborator, Graham Greene, who in the thirties was reviewing films for the *Spectator*. Of *Midshipman Easy* he wrote: 'It is the first film of a new English director, Mr Carol Reed, who has more sense of the cinema than most veteran British directors.'[5] *Laburnum Grove*, he considered, maintained the promise of Reed's début. 'Both films are thoroughly workmanlike and unpretentious, with just the hint of a personal manner which makes one believe that Mr Reed, when he gets the right script, will prove far more than efficient.'[6] Greene, who had yet to switch from criticising films to making them, could scarcely have known how personally involved he would be in this prophecy.

'Workmanlike'. It doesn't sound much, but it's the sort of praise that a professional storyteller like Reed would have appreciated. 'He didn't think of himself as an artist,' commented his son Max. 'He saw himself as a technician. And he saw himself as a man who made films, some of which were good, and some of which were bad, but the whole point was that he made films . . . He would have been the last man in the world who would have said, "I am an artist." '[7]

The system Carol Reed understood best was the one that operated during the Golden Age of Hollywood, and of which the British cinema in the 1930s and 1940s was a pale imitation. His formative experiences were similar to those of American directors like John Ford, William Wyler and Howard

Hawks.* They had begun in films as prop men or gag writers or assistants, and worked on picture after picture before they got the chance to direct themselves. They belonged to the movie *business*, and accepted its rules. They were equally uncomfortable talking about 'art', although they often produced it.

By 1939 Reed had emerged as Britain's leading director, yet – with the one exception of the quota quickie *Talk of the Devil* – all the films he had directed were assignments that producers had given to him. None had been initiated by himself. The difference was that, having established his reputation, now he attracted larger budgets and could be more painstaking.

In 1939 he directed *The Stars Look Down*. Based on A.J. Cronin's novel, the film told the story of the struggle between coal-miners and greedy pit owners. It was a prestigious project: MGM had just enjoyed an enormous critical and commercial success with King Vidor's production of Cronin's novel *The Citadel*. 'I simply took the novel by Cronin,' Reed would later comment. 'I didn't feel particularly about his subject, the nationalisation of mines. One could just as easily make a picture on the opposite side.'[8]

Reed's disavowal of any particular outlook or stance for himself doesn't stand up to a scrutiny of his films but it reflected a deep pride and belief in the system of film-making to which he belonged. When he was asked in 1970 what he thought of the 'auteur theory', he appeared rather baffled by the question. The interviewer had to rephrase it for him:

> 'You've handled such a wide variety of subjects, but are you conscious of any themes or ideas that constantly interest you?'
>
> 'That I myself want to put forward? No. It's always the project. I know that there are great directors, like Visconti and Bergman, who have a certain view of life, but I don't think that a director who knows how

---

* Howard Hawks happened to be directing a film at Shepperton – *I Was a Male War Bride* – at the same time as Carol Reed was making *The Third Man* there.

to put a film together need impose his ideas on the
world. It's another matter, of course, if the ideas are
in the subject. You must always take the author's side
and believe it whilst you're making the picture.'

'What does tend to attract you in the stories you
choose?'

'I tend to look for something exactly opposite from
what I've just done. One can find a comfortable
groove, your best way – but I find that boring.'[9]

There's something rather touching about his old-fashioned
answers, so totally out of keeping with the prejudice of the age.
A cannier man, concerned for his reputation, might have
played along with the interviewer and reinterpreted his
achievements in light of the new orthodoxy. Instead Reed
talked of 'taking the author's side' as if *he* wasn't the author.

Hitchcock – whose films were mostly based on novels and
used scripts invariably written by other men, albeit under his
close guidance – was delighted to stand as the pre-eminent
example of the 'auteur'. He took to the new idea effortlessly, as
François Truffaut's famous interview book with him makes
clear. Reed's commercial success as a director meant that he
came to exert just as much control over his films as Hitchcock.
The difference was that he didn't consider endlessly repeating
himself to be a virtue (even if, none the less, he left his
unmistakable stamp on all he did), and – like the great
Hollywood directors he admired – made light of his own
achievements.

'I don't think a director should stand out,' he declared. 'The
audience should be unconscious that the damned thing's been
directed at all.'[10] Perhaps this explains why he is so little
regarded today. Film critics simply took him at his word.
Watching *Oliver!* recently – the film musical for which Carol
Reed in 1968 finally won the Oscar that he should have
received twenty years previously – it seemed to me that the
director of this film, that few serious critics rate highly,*

---

* In his *Biographical Dictionary of Film* David Thomson dismisses *Oliver!* as 'awful and
unrecognisable as the work of the man who made *Odd Man Out*'.

stood out in the best possible way. The film had all the exuberance and spectacle that one expects of a musical, but also an extraordinary dramatic intensity. The characters were fully realised on the screen in a way that is very rare in any film, let alone a musical. And for those cinephiles who calculate the worth of a director in the number of recurring motifs and themes, these really weren't hard to find.* It would be easy to write an academic study of Reed, but, in some peculiar way, to do so would be to risk diminishing a man whose real genius lay in collaboration.

During the war Reed made *The Young Mr Pitt, Kipps, The Way Ahead* and, together with the American writer/director Garson Kanin, *The True Glory*, the official account of the D-Day landings, which won an Oscar for best documentary. These wartime successes meant that now he was among the handful of British directors who could make almost anything they wanted.

When after *Odd Man Out*, which many critics hailed as the best film ever made, he moved to Sir Alexander Korda's British Lion, it must have seemed like a glamorous career move for Britain's most celebrated film director. But really it was a return to old certainties. Indeed, British Lion had begun life as the company that Edgar Wallace had set up in 1927 to make film versions of his crime stories. Maybe Reed thought it a good omen that he had been in on its beginning. Crucially, Korda was the sort of paternal but autocratic figure under

---

* It suffices to quote from an illuminating letter I received from a reader after the publication of my first book *The Finest Years*: 'Recurring themes in Reed's films: Children, particularly holding balls (*Odd Man Out* and *The Third Man*). Cats: *Girl in the News* – cat playing with a ball of wool, and *Third Man* – Joseph Cotten with cat, and particularly in doorway with Welles. Dustbin rattling in *Odd Man Out* and silver tray in *Oliver!* Parrots: *Fallen Idol* and Joseph Cotten bitten by one in *Third Man*. Dogs: three barking in *Odd Man Out* and Bull's Eye in *Oliver!* Pirouette-like movements: Cyril Cusack with cigarettes in *Odd Man Out*, Porter in *Third Man* after saying, "He was quite dead" in Harry's flat, Ralph Richardson emptying ashtray in the opening of *Fallen Idol*. Most prophetic piece of dialogue is in *Fallen Idol*. After returning from the zoo, Félipe says, "This is a manhole. You can get down to the sewers from here." The above will no doubt be of great psychological interest to some of our own high-flown film critics.'

whose wing Reed had flourished – a creative producer who could encourage the best out of people in a collaborative enterprise and understood the alchemy of creation. It was Korda who established the Carol Reed/Graham Greene partnership when he suggested that Reed should direct an adaptation of Greene's short story 'The Basement Room'.

Together Graham Greene and Carol Reed made films which were far superior to what either achieved apart. Greene wrote location novels in the same way as Reed made location pictures. They both had a powerful sense of setting, entwining real places into their fictional worlds. Both had a feel for estranged, marginal figures. Johnny Macqueen, the wounded – and Catholic – gunman in *Odd Man Out*, could have walked straight out of a Greene novel. They occupied the same terrain: whether or not either appreciated it, Greene wrote the stories that Reed could tell best.

The Fallen Idol and then *The Third Man* are at the very pinnacle of what the old studio system could produce. Reed had the benefit of the accumulated expertise of the team that Korda had brought together at Shepperton, and at every stage of the film-making process the resources to do the job properly. There was a music department, and a scenario department, and an art production department, then, through British Lion, the means to distribute the end product. The people within those departments worked closely together on film after film after film. So there was a continuity and, under the charismatic personality of Sir Alexander Korda, an *esprit de corps*. These were ideal film-making conditions, and Carol Reed took full advantage.

If in subsequent years he never came close to matching *The Third Man*, we shouldn't really be surprised. The old world of the film moguls was at an end. In their place were the faceless corporation and the independent producer. Now directors had to hustle for a picture, they had to be as much businessman as artist. But Reed was pure director, so focused on whatever project was in hand that he couldn't see the world around him.

He was renowned for having his head in the clouds, and there is no shortage of stories which show how out of touch he could be. Once on a trip to New York he was drinking in a bar in Brooklyn, when he heard a wonderful song. It was so marvellous that he thought it had to be used in a film somehow. So he brought back a carload of executives to listen to this song he had discovered. It turned out to be 'Cry' by Johnnie Ray, which had already been Number One for several weeks. Such a man, left to his own devices, was bound to have trouble keeping up with the times.

The collapse of the studio system in the fifties brought to an end the close relationships and continuity out of which the great works of collaborative cinema had emerged. It wasn't just Carol Reed who struggled. In Hollywood John Ford, Frank Capra, William Wyler, Howard Hawks fared little better – they all went on making films well into the 1960s, but none that really compared with their great work of Hollywood's golden age.

In Britain the death of Sir Alexander Korda in 1956 was a particularly bad blow for Reed. Korda made up for his lack of worldliness, and provided the authority and structure that he needed. 'Carol needed whatever a good producer gave him,' commented Guy Hamilton, 'He was never the same after the death of Alex. There was nobody about to guide him in choice of material. He floundered and listened to a lot of silly ladies. I saw him in Hollywood whilst he was making *Agony and Ecstasy*. Very unhappy. Hollywood is a producers' town and Carol could never cope with that horrendous breed ... Funnily enough once he comes back to Europe and John Woolf, a financial and distribution expert and a gentleman, lets him loose on *Oliver!* and never dreams of being anything but supportive and non-interfering everything is sunshine again.'[11]

16

Fifty Years On

Vienna, 22 October 1998. I checked into my hotel and headed straight for the Great Wheel, as newly arrived tourists in Paris make for the Eiffel Tower or in New York for the Empire State Building. Fifty years ago on this day Carol Reed began to film *The Third Man.* Perhaps no other film is so strongly associated with a city. Think of *Casablanca,* for example, and really you're recalling a fantasy concocted on the sound stages of Hollywood. But in Vienna you get an intense sensation of walking through the film – Holly Martins could be just round the corner. Most of the locations are in and around – and under – the Graben and the Kärtnerstrasse, just a gentle stroll from the Sacher Hotel, where both Graham Greene and Holly Martins stayed. You stumble upon them more quickly than you could possibly imagine, as if you really were on a studio backlot. Seeing Vienna as a tourist, you are seeing it pretty much as Graham Greene and Carol Reed would have done – except then the city, immaculate today, was disfigured by bomb damage, and there were no tourists.

The Great Wheel, the Riesenrad, does not so much revolve as jolt from one stationary position to the next. There's something charmingly sluggish about its progress. It will not be hurried, taking a good twenty minutes to get back to where it started. It's no longer the wheel it was. When it was repaired after the war, its load was halved: every other car is missing. They're still doing repairs now. When I arrived two workmen were digging a hole by one of its supporting legs and shovelling spadefuls of earth into a wheelbarrow.

Some of the cars are shut off, reserved for special parties. For 3,600 schillers you can rent your own exclusive cabin for the evening, table and chairs laid on. It must be the only Big Wheel in the world where people turn up not for thrills but for dinner.

In 1997 the Riesenrad celebrated its hundredth birthday. It was built by an Englishman, Walter Basset. He built four others, in London, Blackpool, Chicago and Paris, but they were soon dismantled to make way for some new attraction. In Paris there'd been a terrible accident when one of the cars broke loose, plummeting to the ground and killing everyone inside. It became a music hall ditty. 'When you're sick of your mother-in-law, take her for a ride on the Great Wheel.' Only in Vienna, which holds on so tenaciously to the past, despite wars and collapses of Empire, does the Great Wheel still turn – all four hundred tons of the thing, like a cog in the world's spinning, on an exact north–south axis.

As we clanked to a halt just short of the two-hundred-foot-high summit, a Japanese tourist said in English, 'Flee of income tax, old man. Flee of income tax.' He stuck his camcorder out of the window, pointing it down towards the ground. I imagined him replaying it in Tokyo, and continuing: 'Would you really feel any pity if one of those dots stopped moving for ever?'

But this little piece of movie karaoke was hardly necessary to remind us that we were at one of the epicentres of famous movie lines. Once our carriage had described its circle and returned to the platform again, it would be time to say: 'In Switzerland they had brotherly love, five hundred years of democracy and peace, and what did that produce ...?'

The atmosphere of incipient mimicry and allusion seemed all part of the fun of the fair. Just across the way there was a mini version of the Spanish Riding School – eight or nine overfed ponies trotting around a sawdust ring. When the Prater amusement park was opened last century, it was known as 'Venice in Vienna'. And now, from our Riesenrad summit, we looked down on a giant model of the Chrysler building – Manhattan in Mitteleuropa. Near by, King Kong clung to the 'Zombies' House of Horrors, and a deep, melodramatic voice boomed out terrible warnings to passers-by – although the only words I could make out with my not even schoolboy German were 'Gorilla' and 'Jungefrau'.

Safely on the ground again, I swapped the vulgarity of the amusement park for a stroll up the Hauptallee, the broad avenue of chestnut trees that runs for three miles through the Prater. Joggers and cyclists glided along where once the tanks of the German Army had rolled, retreating westwards out of the city, in a desperate dash for the Reichsbrucke, the last remaining bridge across the Danube. You can see it in the film – the suspension bridge, where Baron Kurtz, Dr Winkler and Popescu turn up for a secretive rendezvous with Harry Lime. About fifteen years ago it collapsed into the Danube with a crash that was heard all over Vienna, its history finally catching up with it.

Crunching through the autumn leaves past the elderly couples sitting on benches and mothers with prams, I found it hard to believe that the place had been the site of so much wartime devastation. On the other side of the avenue, I spotted what looked like a soldier holding a rifle in front of a sculpted stone relief wall. 'Ah,' I thought, 'a monument to the Battle of the Prater, 1945.' I crossed over to find that the rifle was a violin, and the soldier a musician petrified in mid-serenade. The wall relief depicted not a battlefield of square-jawed Red Army heroes, but a ballroom of waltzing couples, the men in tie and tails. It is part of Vienna's charm that statues of musicians should outnumber those of kings and generals by a large number. In the film, after the opening credits, the statue of Strauss in the Stadtpark – close by the entrance to the sewers – is the second image you see.

A group of about forty of us gathered outside the entrance to the Stadtpark U-bahn. I wondered which one was Dr

Timmermann. I had imagined a modern-day Dr Winkel, impossibly precise about details. Instead what I found was a feisty and energetic lady in her late forties, dressed in a pair of jeans and an anorak. I had written to her that I was coming, and had information that she might find interesting. 'You're a guest,' she said, as I was about to hand over 130 schillers, which was the price of the tour.

You only have to look at Vienna's walks guide to appreciate that Dr Timmermann is a formidable lady. She conducts tours every week not just on *The Third Man*, but also on 'The Fascinating World of Crypts, Wine-Cellars, Excavations', ' "Olde Worlde" Vienna in the Shadow of the Cathedral', 'Viennese Art Nouveau: Outcry against the Establishment in Art and Design', 'Jewish Vienna from Stetl to Assimilation' and 'From Imperial Pawn Shop to International Auction House'.

We turned left into the Stadtpark and on to the embankment of the Wienfluss which runs parallel to the railway line. A corporation worker was waiting for us. She opened a door through which we descended down to the level of the river. As we stood in the mouth of the tunnel, Dr Timmermann explained that the main sewer system had been built around the Wien river, but that normally the Wien itself carried no sewage. Only when the two sewers that ran parallel overflowed did their sewage then run into the Wien. As it had been dry for some days now and the water level was low, she assured us that we were unlikely to have a smelly walk.

We followed her into the tunnel. For the first five minutes or so, you could just about make your way by the light from the tunnel mouth, but it curved gradually to the right until it was pitch-black and those of us who had torches switched them on. As we advanced further into the darkness, I felt less like Harry Lime or Holly Martins and more like one of the characters in *Journey to the Centre of the Earth*. After about ten minutes' walk Dr Timmermann stopped at a doorway off the tunnel and invited us to ascend a narrow staircase which spiralled up tightly. At the top we would find ourselves in a kiosk, she told us. Not the one through which Harry Lime escaped into the sewers – that had been in the Am Hof – but another one somewhere near the Secession Building. There were a number of these kiosk exits dotted around Vienna, which had been built just in case the level of the sewers should rise and trap any workers.

I went up last. The stairway was so narrow that I couldn't see how there could be enough space for those people who had reached the kiosk then to get back down past the people still coming up. But just before the last few steps there was a recess in the brickwork into which about two people could squeeze, allowing everyone to work their way round like one of those puzzles with an empty square.

At the top, splinters of daylight revealed that you had reached the surface, but the slits in the side of the kiosk were too high to see out. I stuck my fingers through them and felt drops of rain. The kiosk itself was about two feet across and eight feet high, featureless grey metal. It was like standing inside a huge toilet roll.

I headed back down into the black void at my feet. I thought I had been left alone at the top of the stairs, and my heart skipped a beat when I heard a voice.

'I'm sorry. I don't speak German,' I said, trying to work out where it had come from.

'Can we come down with you?' the voice said in English, 'We don't have any torches.'

'Of course.' I switched on my torch, which revealed, standing in the recess, a woman and two little girls of about five or six.

'They're frightened,' explained the woman.

I said I thought they were terrifically brave – much braver than Orson Welles when he went into the sewers.

The little girls stepped out of the recess and, holding each other's hands, walked down while their English Genie with the Lamp lit up the steps ahead of them. The woman explained how she had seen *The Third Man* at the Burg-Kino, where it plays every week, and decided to go on the tour. Her daughter,

Lea, insisted on coming along with her friend, also called Lea. (So that they didn't get mixed up, they were known as Straight Lea and Curly Lea.)

At the foot of the steps we rejoined the main party and continued down the tunnel. Ten minutes further on we came to another doorway. One by one we passed through it, and there ahead of us was a brick parapet with railings, in effect an aqueduct bridge, under which you could pass if you stooped down very low.

In the film you see the fugitive Harry Lime clamber precariously along the outside of this bridge. Everyone who's seen *The Third Man* must have an image of the scene in their head. Perhaps that's why Jurgen, a twenty-year-old who had come on the tour with his girlfriend, leapt on to the parapet and swung over the railings. As he did so he dropped his torch into the sewage. Everyone laughed, as he ruefully jumped down again without his torch, and his girlfriend muttered some cross words to him in German. I found myself thinking of the warning the TV announcer would make after *Batman*, which I watched when I was small – Batman and the Boy Wonder were professional caped crusaders and knew what they were doing. On no account should we attempt to copy them. Not that we ever paid any more notice than Jurgen.

Dr Timmermann turned around and we followed her back out of the tunnel. We took the stairs back up to the embankment in the Stadtpark and the corporation worker, who had been waiting for us to return, stubbed out her cigarette and locked the gate after us.

'Have you all got U-bahn tickets?' Dr Timmermann asked us. We changed at Karlsplatz, which in Harry Lime's day had been the centre of the black market, and got out at Stephansplatz. We then walked to the various locations of the film, which were to be found conveniently, one after the other, like – as Dr Timmermann put it – the pearls on a necklace.

We stood outside Harry's apartment block – not 'on the edge of Vienna' as Greene described it in the original story, but on the Josefsplatz, opposite a baroque wing of the Hofburg Palace. A long queue for the Spanish Riding School, which was on one side of the square, snaked past a large statue of Josef II sitting on his horse. Here, at No. 5 Josefsplatz, Harry could hardly have lived more centrally. When he opened his curtains in the morning, he would have seen the magnificent façade of the National Library, and above a pageant of statuary cresting its roof parapet: straight ahead Minerva's horses trampling down ignorance and hunger; to the left, Atlas bearing upon his shoulders a massive golden globe. The place suited a man of Harry's style. Four half-naked stone ladies loitered at his doorway as if drawn to his irresistible charm.

Dr Timmermann reminded us of the important scene that had taken place here, the porter of the apartment block telling Holly Martins how Harry had been killed in a traffic accident, and how two friends of his had carried him across to the statue. 'And there was a third man . . .'

We crowded the doorway, spilling out on to the road as we listened. 'Be careful not to get run over like Harry Lime,' said Dr Timmermann as a fiacre nearly flattened one of our number. It was a standard joke but in the narrow streets of Vienna getting run over was a real danger.

We walked on up the Josefsplatz, under an archway and into the Michaelerplatz. Here Sergeant Paine and Major Calloway had hidden behind a fountain, lying in wait for Harry Lime. A few feet further on, Hercules was clubbing to death some poor animal by the entrance to the Hofburg.

We turned off Kohlmarkt, and Dr Timmermann pointed at some grilled windows in a bare expanse of nondescript and newly whitewashed wall. 'Do you remember Harry's shadow on the wall when he runs away from Martins? This is the wall.' She sighed sadly. 'What a pity you weren't here two months ago. It was falling to pieces, but it was just like in the film.'

We'd been walking for about an hour and a half. We looked at some more locations – the Am Hof, where Harry disappeared down into the sewers, the block of flats in which Anna lived – but we were all now waiting for just one thing.

We walked up Herrengasse and Freyung. We climbed a steep cobbled path up to Molker Bastei – a bit of old rampart that had somehow eluded Franz Josef's bulldozers when he tore down the city walls. And then there it was: the Doorway. And opposite, the house whose windows had lit up with Martins' shouting. 'What kind of a spy do you think you are, satchel-foot?' Passers-by must have thought we were mad, staring at an empty doorway in silence, but each of us in our heads was rerunning that magic moment – the impish smile of Harry Lime caught in the light.

'I have one last surprise for you,' said Dr Timmermann. She led us down a flight of steps, and into a shop. All forty or so of us marched past a shop assistant examining a till roll and down several flights of stairs. We came into a cellar. When Vienna was a walled city, Dr Timmermann explained, space was at such a premium that the Viennese dug down, building cellars beneath their houses. Over the years, as people sought extra storage space, they would buy the cellar next door and connect it to their own. Gradually, by this spontaneous process, a subterranean network developed. In the various crises that over the years affected the city it was as much through the cellars as the sewers that fugitives would make their escape.

Waiting in the cellar was Helmut, a young zither-player, who welcomed us with 'The Third Man Theme' and 'The Café Mozart Waltz'.

After the tour I had a drink with Dr Timmermann in a nearby café. Dr Timmermann was writing her own book about *The Third Man*, but our initial wariness of each other melted in the recognition of our mutual enthusiasm for the film. We rivalled each other only in our eagerness to reveal facts that the other might not know. Dr Timmermann – or Brigitte as I came to know her – told me triumphantly how after years of looking in the Zentralfriedhof (which contains about two million graves) she had finally discovered where Harry Lime was buried. I said that I would go and pay my respects the next day. She took out a map of the cemetery to give me directions, spreading it out over the beer mats.

We talked for hours. It was nearly midnight when we left the bar. 'Where's your hotel?' she asked.

'The Hotel Post in Fleischmarkt.'

'How funny. I have a key to one of these cellars I was talking about and it's just by your hotel. I'll show you if you like.'

We reached Fleischmarkt and Brigitte led me to a side entrance in the apartment block opposite the Hotel Post. We followed a sign to 'Der Keller' and descended several flights of stairs. We then walked along a passageway and Brigitte pushed a door at the end.

'Fourteenth century,' she said, as she switched on some lights. There was a musty smell of earth. Ahead of us beneath a vaulted brick ceiling was a long dining table, flanked on either side by a row of grilled alcoves, each stacked with bottles of wine. Brigitte explained that this particular cellar had been bought by a drinking fraternity. She then showed me the tunnels that connected with other cellars, so low that you had to stoop down to pass through them.

'This one goes to your hotel, but it's been bricked off, because they don't want anyone to get in without them knowing.'

We went through another passageway, opened a door, and suddenly, as if we had walked from one movie set to another, there was loud music and bright lights and we were pushing our way past crowded tables. We reached the street. Over our heads was a neon sign: 'Frank's American Bar'.

How stupid of Harry to get trapped in the sewers, I thought after I had said goodbye to Brigitte and returned to my hotel – by the front entrance. He should have used the cellars instead.

More people lie in Vienna's Zentralfriedhof than are currently alive in the city. Built in the middle of the last century, it is where everyone, rich or poor, goes to be buried. At the main gate, there is what must without question be the world's largest wreath emporium – row after row of flower-covered market stalls, where you can get whatever you need, whether you're burying your old aunt or a king.

At first the Viennese were sceptical about this vast new cemetery. They didn't like the idea of having to go all the way to a distant suburb to be buried. After the gates had been open for some years and there was still an embarrassing shortfall of corpses, the City authorities realised that there would have to be some kind of an attraction. So they dug up the bodies of Beethoven and Schubert and put them near the entrance together with a memorial to Mozart.* The trick worked. Suddenly the Zentralfriedhof was fashionable.

The celebrity plots are clustered between the main entrance and a huge domed church some two hundreds yards or so further on, the Dr-Karl-Lueger-Kirke. One moment you seem to be walking past the headstones of the entire repertory company of the Burg Theater, circa 1930, next the pre-Anschluss cabinet, uncannily reunited in death. It's impossible not to admire the contrivance. If death itself cannot be cheated, at least a little bit of re-digging can lend it a pleasing aspect. So the re-diggings that would attend Harry Lime's admission to the cemetery were nothing new.

Brigitte had lent me a map and marked with a cross where Harry was buried. She also gave me a still from the film of Trevor Howard as Major Calloway standing by a distinctive black tombstone, with the name ELCHINGER and the date, 1913, displayed in a diamond. That was what I was to look out for.

I walked away from the celebrities to the far side of the church. On my right there was a Garden of Remembrance for the soldiers of the Red Army. Two granite warriors, bearing flag and rifle, guarded the pathway to an obelisk memorial. Stone after stone bore the same date – XIII.4.1945 – the bloodiest day in the fighting for Vienna.

On the other side of the road were buried the civilians. One inscription leapt out at me: 'Anna Schmidt, 1928'. There were

---

* As he'd been buried in a mass grave in the Sankt Marxer Friedhof, his remains were impossible to identify.

probably more Schmidts buried here than any other cemetery in the world, but I couldn't help wondering if Graham Greene, who would have trodden the same path, had also noticed this name, and chosen it for the girl in his story.

I had my map, I even had a reference number – gruppe 43A, reihe 14 – but it still took me ages to find where Lime had been buried. Whatever their differences close-up, tombstones look more or less alike from a distance. But just as I imagined having shamefully to confess my failure to Brigitte, suddenly I saw ELCHINGER, and opposite was Harry's plot.

It didn't bear his name of course, but that of the person whose resting-place had been briefly borrowed: JOHANN GRÜN. As was clear now, from just reading the dates on a few inscriptions, the film-makers had a lot of fresh burial plots to choose from in the autumn of 1948. What drew them to this one, I imagined, were the cypress trees that formed such a striking backdrop. I took out my camera and, as I tried to reproduce the scene, looking closely at the Trevor Howard still, I found myself mildly irritated by the fifty years of crosses that had been added since.

Months later I learnt that the scene in which Harry is dug up was shot at Shepperton. Having looked at the film many times now, I still find it impossible to distinguish between what is real and what is false. Lime's missing body was not the only deception to take place in the Zentralfriedhof.

None the less, visiting with a camera gives some idea of the great sense of opportunity the film-makers must have felt. Like me, they had turned up not to respect the dead but to get some good pictures. A little beyond Harry's grave runs the road where Holly Martins waits for Anna at the end of the film. You can identify it by an obelisk in the distance. In real life there would have been no reason for Anna to go as far as this road. After Harry's funeral, she would simply have turned around and walked back the way she had come past the church to the main entrance. But the obelisk must have caught Reed's attention and he decided to put it in the film.

I went up to photograph this scene of one of the cinema's

most famous endings. I framed the obelisk, then walked back a little further, then framed the obelisk again, then walked back even further. There was something seductive about the road with its lines converging on some far point lost in the autumn rain. You wanted as much of that distance as you could get, not just a short stretch. But watching the film again some time later, I realised that it wasn't quite as I imagined. Anna in the distance walks not from the obelisk, but towards it. And I wondered what had really happened.

The End

Cemetery street. Day location.
ANNA *is on her way to the tram stop walking down the*
long dreary road.
Car. Back projection.
MARTINS: Wait a minute. Let me out . . .
CALLOWAY: Well, there's not much time.
MARTINS: I can't just leave . . .
CALLOWAY *slows the car and brings it to a stop.*
Cemetery street location.
CALLOWAY: Be sensible, Martins.
MARTINS (*as he stands beside the jeep*): I haven't got a
sensible name . . . Calloway.
He begins to walk back down the road. CALLOWAY
turns and watches. ANNA *is approaching.* MARTINS
stops and waits for her. She reaches him and he seeks
in vain for a word. He makes a gesture with his
hand, and she pays no attention, walking right past
him and on into the distance. MARTINS *follows her*
with his eyes. From outside our vision we can hear a
car horn blown again and again.

The actors and film crew turned up at the cemetery at about
nine in the morning. It was a freezing cold day in early
December. They'd been shooting virtually round the clock for
many weeks now and tempers were frayed. They went to the
road just beyond the group of graves where they had shot
Lime's funeral, the longest avenue in the cemetery. Reed told
the cameraman, Hans Schneeberger, to put the camera low

down in the middle of the road. He crouched down himself to peer through, and groaned because it was Schneeberger's old Eclair and he couldn't see a thing through the viewfinder.

He told Joseph Cotten to stand by an old cart not far from the *Gärtnerei*, the cemetery's garden centre. Perhaps it was then that he noticed the dead leaves, which would have been piled high at this time of year.

'It would be marvellous if we had dead leaves falling,' he said. So a ladder was found and a couple of prop men with a bag of leaves climbed high enough into the tree not to be picked up by the camera.

Now they were ready to shoot Alida Valli walking up the cemetery path. She was taken back some distance, but Reed said, 'Further back, further back.' So she went even further back, but he still wasn't satisfied.

Guy Hamilton, whose job it was to communicate to Valli when and from where she should set off, lost his patience. He jumped into Calloway's jeep and caught up with Valli. 'Hop in,' he told her and together they drove to the very end of the road. She got out and he told her: 'Darling, hang about. When you see me drop the handkerchief, start walking.' He turned the jeep around and drove back to the unit.

'What's Alida doing down there?' Reed asked.

'Carol, tell me when you've finished fucking about, just say action, and I'll send Alida off, and then when you consider her to be far enough or near enough away turn the camera over, and end of story, right? Couldn't be more simple.'

So Reed said action. Hamilton dropped his handkerchief and Valli, little more than a dot in the distance, began to walk towards the camera. They waited for her to get closer.

'Do you know,' said Reed, 'We could use this for the end titles, I mean she's coming along, and then we'd run the end titles. How long are the end titles?'

Only Schneeberger seemed to know. 'Forty-eight metres,' he said. The English crew argued over how many feet there were to the metre and how many seconds. Someone took out a Jackson Rose to find out.

Joseph Cotten asked if he could light a cigarette, and up in the tree the prop men were beginning to run out of leaves.

'Slow down on the leaves!'

'If we run the credit titles,' Reed joked, 'you'll soon know who stayed to watch the end of the fucking picture, won't you?' In those days, once the end credits began to run, everyone hurried out of the cinema to avoid having to stand for 'God Save the King'.

The camera, trained on the road, continued running. Still Valli was just a tiny figure, and as they waited for her Reed began to realise the permutations. Looking down the road, he said: 'We could fade out now and you'll never know whether they . . .'

And Anna continued walking.

Credits

A London Films production distributed by British Lion Film Corporation. Presented by Alexander Korda and David O. Selznick.

Producer and Director	Carol Reed
Original story and screenplay	Graham Greene
Photography	Robert Krasker
Music	Anton Karas
Art Director	Vincent Korda
Editor	Oswald Hafenrichter
Associate Producer	Hugh Perceval
Assistant Director	Guy Hamilton
2nd Assistant Director	Jack Causey
3rd Assistant Director	Jackie Green
Assistant to Associate Producer	Bob Dunbar
Additional Photography	John Wilcox
	Stan Pavey
	Hans Schneeberger
Assistants to Art Director	John Hawkesworth
	Joseph Bato
	Ferdinand Bellan
	James Sawyer
Camera Operators	E. Scaife
	Denys Coop
	Monty Berman
Set dresser	Dario Simoni
Continuity	Peggy McClafferty

Assistant continuity	Angela Allen
Story Advisor	Peter Smollett
Additional dialogue	Jerome Chodorov
	Mabbie Poole
Austrian Advisors	Elizabeth Montagu
	Paul Martin
Production Manager	T.S. Lyndon-Haynes
Sound Supervisor	John Cox
Sound Recording	Bert Ross
	Red Law
	George Adams
Sound Editing	Jack Drake
Assistant Cutters	Peter Taylor
	David Eady
	Ken Behrens
	Michael Coton
Make-up	George Frost
Assistant Make-up	Peter Evans
Hairdressing	Joe Shear
Assistant Hairdresser	Iris Tilley
Wardrobe Supervisor	Ivy Baker
Wardrobe Master	George Murray
Wardrobe Assistants	Gene Hornsby
	Dick Richardson
Focus operators	G. Meldrum
	J. Kotze
Clappers	A. McCabe
Loader	J. Bicknell
Sound camera operator	J. Dooley
Sound boom operator	J. Davies
Buyer	George Durant
Floor props	Syd Leggett
Floor electrician	H. Mackay
Stills	Len Lee
Publicist	Enid Jones
Production Secretary	Teresa Deans
Driver	T. Goodrun

Cast

Holly Martins	Joseph Cotten
Anna Schmidt	Alida Valli
Harry Lime	Orson Welles
Major Calloway	Trevor Howard
The Porter	Paul Hoerbiger
Baron Kurtz	Ernst Deutsch
Dr Winkel	Erich Ponto
Popescu	Siegfried Breuer
Anna's landlady	Hedwig Bleibtreu
Sergeant Paine	Bernard Lee
Crabbin	Wilfrid Hyde-White
The Porter's Wife	Annie Rosar
Hansl	Herbert Halbik
Brodsky	Alexis Chesnakov
Hall Porter at Sacher's	Paul Hardtmuth
Hansl's Father	Frederick Schreicker
Winkel's housekeeper	Jenny Werner
Barman at the Casanova	Leo Bieber
Doorman at the Casanova	Fritz Weiss
Head waiter at the Casanova	Martin Miller
Waiter in Kärtnerstrasse bar	Erich Pohlmann
Passport Officer	Reed de Rouen
Nurse	Lily Kann
Driver	Thomas Gallagher
Diners at the Casanova	Madge Brindley
	Jack Faint
Actors at Josefstadt Theatre	Karl Stepanek
	Hannah Norbert
Crabbin's guest	Paula Breese
Young Austrian	Fritz Krenn
Popescu's heavies	Harry Belcher
	Michael Connor
International Patrol (A)	Jack Arrow
	Reg Morris
	Stephen Gray

	Duncan Ryder
International Patrol (B)	Brooks Kyle
	Ray Browne
	Arthur Hall
	Howard Leighton
International Patrol (C)	Gordon Tanner
	Michael Godfrey
	Guy Du Morceau
	Arthur Barrett
International Patrol (D)	Paul Carpenter
	Geoffrey Keene
	Vernon Greeves

Length: British Lion release, 104 minutes; Selznick release, 93 minutes.

Chronology

1948

26 January: Graham Greene contracted to write 'an original story suitable for the production of a cinematograph film'.

11 February: Greene arrives in Vienna, where he stays at the Sacher Hotel.

17 February: Greene meets *The Times* correspondent Peter Smollett.

2 March–24 April: Greene writes *The Third Man* in Italy.

7 May: Carol Reed and Alexander Korda leave for Bermuda, where they join David Selznick on a yachting holiday.

14 May: David Selznick and Alexander Korda sign a deal in New York to co-produce four films, including *The Third Man*.

18 May: Carol Reed and Alexander Korda arrive back in England.

18 June: Graham Greene and Carol Reed arrive in Vienna, where they spend two weeks working on the script.

8 July: First draft script of *The Third Man* completed.

14 July: Joseph Cotten arrives in England to work on Hitchcock's *Under Capricorn*.

8–19 August: Graham Greene and Carol Reed discuss first draft script with David Selznick in California.

8 September: Jerome Chodorov arrives in London to write the American dialogue for the film.

20 September: Final script finished.

16 October: Carol Reed departs for Vienna.

22 October: First night of principal photography.

23 October: Alexander Korda and David Selznick meet in New York to patch up differences over the script.

31 October: Joseph Cotten arrives in Vienna.

18 November: Orson Welles walks to and from the Great Wheel in the Prater.

8 December: Joseph Cotten finishes in Vienna.

11 December: Unit party for Viennese crew.

15 December: British crew return to England.

29 December: Filming recommences at Isleworth Studios.

1949

6 January: Filming transfers to Shepperton Studios.

16 January: Orson Welles arrives in London from Paris for a week's work.

18 March: Joseph Cotten finishes filming at Shepperton Studios.

25 March: Cotten leaves for America on board the *Queen Mary*.

31 March: Completion of principal photography. Alida Valli's last day.

1 June: Anton Karas begins to work on the music. He will spend ten weeks on the film.

27 July: Cutting-room fire destroys several reels of the rough cut.

25 August: David Selznick, who is in London, sees the film for the first time.

1 September: Joseph Cotten wins best actor award at the Venice international film festival for *Portrait of Jennie*.

2 September: *The Third Man* opens in London at the Plaza, Piccadilly.

12 September: David Selznick begins to edit the American version.

17 September: *The Third Man* is awarded the Grand Prix at the Cannes film festival.

31 October: The film goes on general release.

16 November: Anton Karas begins an engagement at the Empress Club, London.

1950

2 February: After several postponements, the film finally opens in America at the Victoria Theater, New York.

1951

29 March: At the Academy Awards ceremony in Hollywood Robert Krasker wins Oscar for best black-and-white photography; the film had received nominations for direction (Carol Reed) and editing (Oswald Hafenrichter).

Notes

1: 'Mixing Fact with Fiction'

1 *The Third Man and the Fallen Idol* (Penguin Books, 1971), p.9.
2 Letter to Catherine Walston, 30 September 1948, quoted in Norman Sherry, *The Life of Graham Greene*, vol. 2: 1939–1955 (Jonathan Cape, 1994), p.242.
3 Guy Hamilton, interview, 15 October 1997.
4 Elizabeth Montagu, 28 October 1997.
5 London Film Productions Archive, BFI Library Special Collection, LFP C/044(iii).
6 Letter agreement (drawn up after Smollett's engagement), 24 July 1948, London Film Productions Archive, BFI Library Special Collection, LFP A/19(iv-d).
7 London Film Productions Archive, BFI Special Collection, LFP A/19(iv-d).

2: 'Bombed About a Bit'

1 *The Times*, 16 November 1946.
2 Jan Morris, *Fifty Years of Europe: An Album* (Viking, 1997), p.331.
3 Gordon Brook-Shepherd, *The Austrians: A Thousand-Year Odyssey* (HarperCollins, 1996), pp.329–30.
4 Patrick Howarth, *My God, Soldiers* (Hutchinson, 1989), p.232.
5 *Austrians*, p.343.
6 Karl Vocelka, *Trümmerjahre Wien 1945–1949* (Jugend und Volk, 1985), p.11.
7 'Vienna Today', *March of Time*, 1952.
8 *Journey to Vienna* (J.M. Dent, 1950), p.114.

9 ibid., p.165.

10 ibid., p.183.

11 *Guardian*, 11 March 1950.

12 Gordon Brook-Shepherd, interview, 6 January 1999.

13 *The Times*, 26 May 1948.

14 ibid., 4 April 1950.

3: 'Then Along Came This Silly American!'

1 Jenia Reissar to David Selznick, 21 May 1948, Harry Ransom Center, David O. Selznick Collection, box 740, file 2.

2 Alexander Korda to David Selznick, 8 June 1948, Selznick, 915, 5.

3 Guy Hamilton, interview, 15 October 1997.

4 *The Pleasure Dome: The Collected Film Criticism 1935–40* (Oxford University Press, 1980), p.3.

5 ibid.

6 'The Third Man: Remarks of David Selznick in Bermuda', n.d., Carol Reed Papers, BFI Library Special Collection.

7 *The Third Man and The Fallen Idol* (Penguin, 1971), p.11.

8 Guardian Lecture at National Film Theatre, printed in the *Graham Greene Film Reader: Mornings in the Dark*, ed. David Parkinson (Carcanet, 1993), p.557.

9 Interview in Charles Thomas Samuels, *Encountering Directors* (Putnam & Sons, 1972), pp.169–70.

10 Alexander Korda to David Selznick, 2 July 1948, Selznick, 915, 5.

11 Carol Reed to David Selznick, 8 July 1948, Selznick, 586, 7.

12 Barbara Keon to David Selznick, 16 July 1948, Selznick, 586, 7.

13 David Selznick to Barbara Keon, 17 July 1948, Selznick, 3042, 15.

14 Ann Harris to Barbara Keon, 13 August 1948, Selznick, 3133, 2.

15 ibid.

16 'The Third Man: Remarks of David Selznick in Bermuda', n.d., Carol Reed papers, BFI Special Collection.

17 Contract with 20th Century-Fox, 27 June 1947, London Film Productions Archive, BFI Library Special Collection, LFP, 20th Century-Fox file.

18 David Selznick to Jenia Reissar, 16 June 1948, Selznick 915, 5.

19 David Selznick to Carol Reed, 22 May 1948, Selznick 915, 5.

20 David Selznick to Jenia Reissar, 30 June 1948, Selznick 915, 5.

21 David Selznick to Jenia Reissar, 16 June 1948, Selznick 915, 5.

22 David Selznick memorandum, 3 June 1948, Selznick 916, 7.

23 David Selznick to Jenia Reissar, 21 September 1948, Selznick 740, 4.

24 Sir Alexander Korda to David Selznick, 23 September 1948, Selznick 740, 3.

25 David Selznick to Milton Kramer, 13 October 1948, Selznick 586, 7.

26 David Selznick to Milton Kramer, 9 October 1948, Selznick 915, 7.

27 All quotes from the conference notes come from the copy in the Carol Reed Papers, BFI Library Special Collection.

28 *The Pleasure Dome*, p.3.

29 Sir Alexander Korda to David Selznick, 29 July 1948, Selznick 915, 6.

30 David Selznick to Sir Alexander Korda, 30 July 1948, Selznick 915, 6.

31 Copy in Carol Reed Papers, BFI Library Special Collection.

32 Joseph Breen to David Selznick, 22 October 1948, Selznick 916, 6.

33 David Selznick to Jenia Reissar, 13 August 1948, Selznick 740, 4.

34 ibid.

35 Interview, 7 September 1998.

36 Jenia Reissar to David Selznick, 5 October 1948, Selznick 740, 4.

37 Sir Alexander Korda to David Selznick, 7 October 1948, Selznick 915, 7.

38 David Selznick memorandum, 9 October 1948, Selznick 915, 7.

39 Jenia Reissar to David Selznick, 29 September 1948, Selznick 586, 7.

40 Selznick's cable quoted in Jenia Reissar letter to Sir Alexander Korda, 6 October 1948, Selznick, 586, 7.

41 Sir Alexander Korda to David Selznick, 7 October 1948.

42 Jenia Reissar to David Selznick, 11 October 1948, Selznick 740, 6.

43 Jenia Reissar to Milton Kramer, 18 October 1948, Selznick 740, 6.

44 Jenia Reissar to Milton Kramer, 17 October 1948, Selznick 740, 6.

45 David Selznick to Betty Goldsmith, 16 October 1948, Selznick 586, 7.

46 Jenia Reissar to David Selznick, 19 October 1948, 740, 6.

47 David Selznick memorandum, 19 October 1948, Selznick 915, 7.

48 David Selznick to Jenia Reissar, 19 October 1948, Selznick 915, 7.

49 Sir Alexander Korda to Rosemary Clifford, 3 December 1948, Selznick 916, 6.

4: On Location

1 London Film Productions Archive, BFI Library Special Collection, LFP A/19(i-a).

2 Guy Hamilton, interview, 15 October 1997.

3 ibid.
4 ibid.
5 Elizabeth Montagu, interview, 28 October 1997.
6 Jenia Reissar to David Selznick, 16 November 1948, Selznick 740, 7.
7 David Selznick to Louis Lewis, 22 November 1948, Selznick 916, 6.
8 Rosemary Clifford to David Selznick, 29 November 1948, Selznick 740, 7.
9 Jenia Reissar to David Cunynghame, 7 January 1949, Selznick 741, 1.
10 Colonel John Codrington to Jenia Reissar, 30 September 1948, Selznick 740, 3.
11 Elizabeth Montagu, interview, 28 October 1997.
12 *Vanity Will Get You Somewhere* (Columbus Books, 1987), p.73.
13 Jenia Reissar to Richard Hungate, 11 October 1948, Selznick 740, 6.
14 Guy Hamilton, interview, 15 October 1997.
15 Bob Dunbar, interview, 14 February 1995.
16 Guy Hamilton, interview, 15 October 1997.

5: Stealing the Limelight

1 Michael Korda, *Charmed Lives: A Family Romance* (Random House, 1979), pp.223–5.
2 London Film Productions Archive, BFI Library Special Collection, LFP C/128(i).
3 Orson Welles and Peter Bogdanovich, *This is Orson Welles*, ed. Jonathan Rosenbaum (HarperCollins, 1993), pp.107–8.
4 London Film Productions Archive, BFI Library Special Collection, 20th Century-Fox file.
5 Barbara Leaming, *Orson Welles* (Weidenfeld, 1985), p.362.
6 David Selznick to Milton Kramer, 4 October 1948, Selznick 915, 7.
7 Record of a telephone conversation with Tristram Owen, legal adviser of London Film Productions, dated 29 June 1949, Selznick 741, 5.
8 Memorandum from Tristram Owen to Harold Boxall, 8 April 1948, and memorandum from David Cunynghame to Harold Boxall, 30 April 1948, London Film Productions Archive, BFI Library Special Collection, C/128(i) and C/128(ii).
9 Letter from H. Lewis of London Films to Robert White & Sons, 17 January 1950, London Film Productions Archive, BFI Special Collection, LFP C/128(iii).

10 Guy Hamilton, interview, 15 October 1997.

11 John Hawkesworth, interview, 7 April 1997.

12 Bob Dunbar, interview, 14 February 1995.

13 Guy Hamilton, interview, 15 October 1997.

14 Elizabeth Montagu, interview, 28 October 1997.

15 *Daily Express*, 3 February 1949.

16 *This is Orson Welles*, p.220.

17 Peter Cowie, *A Ribbon of Dreams: The Cinema of Orson Welles* (Tantivy, 1973), p.210.

18 Peter Noble, *The Fabulous Orson Welles* (Hutchinson, 1956), p.219.

19 Charles Higham, *Orson Welles: Rise and Fall of an American Genius* (St Martin's Press, 1985), pp.312–13.

20 Bob Dunbar, interview, 14 February 1995.

6: In the Studio

1 *Cinema Studio*, 5 January 1949.

2 ibid, 12 January 1949.

3 Interview, 7 April 1997.

4 *Cinema Studio*, 19 January 1949.

5 Interview, 7 April 1997.

6 Guy Hamilton, interview, 15 October 1997.

7 Norman Spencer, interview, 31 March 1998.

8 *Film Industry*, 24 March 1949.

9 Selznick 916, 5.

10 David Selznick to Sir Alexander Korda, 22 December 1948, Selznick 916, 3.

11 Interview, 15 October 1997.

12 Korda told Selznick that he was going to ask Cotten in a cable dated 17 December 1948, Selznick 916, 3.

13 Record of a telephone conversation between Jenia Reissar and Joseph Cotten, 11 February 1949, Selznick 741, 2.

14 Notes for a telephone conversation with Daniel O'Shea, Selznick 741, 2.

15 A letter from Ingram Fraser to Carol Reed, discussing these instructions, 10 December 1948, Carol Reed Papers, BFI Library Special Collection.

16 ibid.

17 Carol Reed to Ingram Fraser, 12 February 1949, Carol Reed Papers, BFI Library Special Collection.

7: 'You'll Never Teach These Austrians to be Good Citizens!'

1 Berkley, George, *Vienna and Its Jews: The Tragedy of Success, 1880s–1980s* (Abt Books, 1988), p.348.
2 Quoted in Goswin Doerfler, *Focus on Film*, March 1978, p.40.
3 London Film Productions Archive, BFI Special Library, LFP A/19(ii).
4 Leni Riefenstahl, *The Sieve of Time: The Memoirs of Leni Riefenstahl* (Quartet, 1992), pp.57–8.

8: The Fourth Man

1 Guy Hamilton, interview, 15 October 1997.
2 David Eady, interview, 3 June 1998.
3 *News Review*, 9 March 1950.
4 Guy Hamilton, interview, 15 October 1997.
5 *Sunday Mercury*, 23 October 1949.
6 28 October 1949.
7 *Gramophone*, December 1949.
8 *Melody Maker* 17 December 1949.
9 *New Musical Express*, 2 December 1949.
10 *Melody Maker* 10 December 1949.
11 28 October 1949.
12 Selznick 916, 8.
13 Quoted in Rudy Behlmer (ed.), *Memo from David O. Selznick* (Macmillan, 1973), p. 391.
14 Robert Gillham to Robert Dann, 29 November 1949, Selznick 916, 10.
15 Elizabeth Montagu, interview, 28 October 1997.
16 15 November 1949.
17 *Daily Express*, 17 November 1949.
18 ibid., 20 November 1949.
19 *Trinidad Guardian*, 18 December 1949.
20 Memorandum, 28 December 1949, Selznick 916, 9.
21 Elizabeth Montagu, interview, 28 October 1997.
22 *New York Herald Tribune*, 26 February 1950.
23 Guy Hamilton, interview, 15 October 1997.

9: Falling Out

1 David Selznick to Jenia Reissar, 10 July 1949, 916, 6.
2 David Selznick to Vanguard Films, 27 July 1949, Selznick 916, 6.
3 Bob Gillham to David Selznick, 16 September 1949, Selznick 916, 6.
4 David Selznick memorandum, 15 September 1949, Selznick 916, 6.
5 ibid.
6 Jenia Reissar to Graham Greene, 17 October 1949, Selznick 916, 6.
7 Graham Greene to Jenia Reissar, 18 October 1949, Selznick 916, 6.
8 Sir Alexander Korda to David Selznick, 19 October 1949, Selznick 742, 3.
9 David Selznick to Jenia Reissar, 20 October 1949, Selznick 916, 6.
10 Jenia Reissar to Sir Alexander Korda, 24 October 1949, Selznick 916, 6.
11 Sir Alexander Korda to David Selznick, 28 October 1949, Selznick 742, 4.
12 David Selznick to Sir Alexander Korda, 14 November 1949, Selznick 742, 5.
13 David Selznick, statement for attorneys, 26 November 1949, Selznick 742, 6.
14 David Selznick to Jenia Reissar, 7 January 1950, Selznick 916, 6.
15 Sir Alexander Korda to David Selznick, 28 November 1949, Selznick 742, 6.
16 Memorandum to Daniel O'Shea, 28 November 1949, Selznick 916, 6.
17 David Selznick to Jenia Reissar, 11 February 1950, Selznick 916, 6.
18 David Selznick to Carol Reed, via a cable to Jenia Reissar, 5 January 1950, Selznick 916, 6.
19 Quoted in a cable from David Selznick to Jenia Reissar, 7 January 1950, Selznick 916, 6.
20 Orson Welles and Peter Bogdanovich, *This is Orson Welles*, ed. Jonathan Rosenbaum (HarperCollins, 1993), p.222.

11: 'Pardon Me If I Rave!'

1 *The Times*, 3 September 1949.
2 10 September 1949.
3 2 September 1949.
4 8 September 1949.
5 21 October 1949.

6 *Cinématographe française*, 29 October 1949.

7 30 September 1949.

8 *Edinburgh Evening Dispatch*, 7 January 1950.

9 David Selznick to Jenia Reissar, 16 September 1949, Selznick 916, 6.

10 Dudley Steele to Daniel O'Shea, 31 March 1950.

12: The Return of the Third Man

1 David Thomson, *Suspects* (Secker & Warburg, 1985), p.102.

13: The Heart of the Matter

1 Kim Philby, *My Silent War* (Panther, 1979), p.50.

2 Otto John, *Twice through the Lines* (Futura, 1974), p.265.

3 Foreword to Kim Philby, *My Silent War* (Panther, 1979), p.9.

4 Gordon Brook-Shepherd, interview, 6 January 1999.

5 Genrikh Borovik, *The Philby Files: The Secret Life of the Master Spy – KGB Archives Revealed*, ed. Philip Knightley (Little, Brown, 1994), pp.137–8.

6 ibid., p.139.

7 See Norman Sherry, *The Life of Graham Greene*, vol. 2: 1939–1955 (Jonathan Cape, 1994), p.244.

8 Graham Greene, *Ways of Escape* (Bodley Head, 1980), p.126.

9 Anthony Cave Brown, *Treason in the Blood: H. St. John Philby, Kim Philby and the Spy Case of the Century* (Robert Hale, 1995), p.601.

10 ibid., p.602.

11 Quoted in Patrick Seale and Maureen McConville, *Philby: The Long Road to Moscow* (Hamish Hamilton, 1973), p.102.

12 ibid.

13 *My Silent War* (Panther, 1979), p.16.

14 *The Third Man and the Fallen Idol* (Penguin, 1971), p.11.

14: The Little Duke

1 *A Sort of Life* (Bodley Head, 1971), p.86.

2 ibid., pp.79–80.

3 ibid., p.80.

4 Quoted in Norman Sherry, *The Life of Graham Greene*, vol. 1: 1904–1939 (Jonathan Cape, 1989), p.179.

15: The Storyteller

1 Interview, 15 October 1997.
2 ibid.
3 Richard Schickel, *The Men Who Made the Movies* (Atheneum, 1975), p.101.
4 Quoted in Nicholas Wapshott, *The Man Between: A Biography of Carol Reed* (Chatto & Windus, 1990), p.98.
5 *The Graham Greene Film Reader: Mornings in the Dark*, ed. David Parkinson (Carcanet, 1993), p.61.
6 ibid., p.125.
7 Max Reed, interview, 23 June 1998.
8 Charles Thomas Samuels, *Encountering Directors* (Putnam & Sons, 1972), p.174.
9 ibid., p.166.
10 ibid., p.165.
11 Guy Hamilton, letter, 10 July 1998.

Bibliography

Berkley, George E., *Vienna and Its Jews: The Tragedy of Success, 1880s–1980s*, Abt Books, 1988

Borovik, Genrikh, *The Philby Files: The Secret Life of the Master Spy – KGB Archives Revealed*, ed. Philip Knightley, Little Brown, 1994

Brook-Shepherd, Gordon, *The Austrians: A Thousand-Year Odyssey*, HarperCollins, 1996

Cave Brown, Anthony, *Treason in the Blood: H. St. John Philby, Kim Philby and the Spy Case of the Century*, Robert Hale, 1995

Cotten, Joseph, *Vanity Will Get You Somewhere*, Columbus Books, 1987

Greene, Graham, *A Sort of Life*, Bodley Head, 1971

—*The Third Man and the Fallen Idol*, Penguin Books, 1971

—*The Pleasure Dome: The Collected Film Criticism 1935–40*, Oxford University Press, 1980

—*Ways of Escape*, Bodley Head, 1980

—*Graham Greene Film Reader: Mornings in the Dark*, ed. David Parkinson, Carcanet, 1993

Henrey, Mrs Robert, *Journey to Vienna*, J.M. Dent, 1950

Higham, Charles, *Orson Welles: Rise and Fall of an American Genius*, St Martin's Press, 1985

Howarth, Patrick, *My God, Soldiers*, Hutchinson, 1989

John, Otto, *Twice through the Lines*, Futura, 1974

Korda, Michael, *Charmed Lives: A Family Romance*, Random House, 1979

Leaming, Barbara, *Orson Welles*, Weidenfeld, 1985

Noble, Peter, *The Fabulous Orson Welles*, Hutchinson, 1956

Philby, Kim, *My Silent War*, with introduction by Graham Greene, Panther, 1979

Riefenstahl, Leni, *The Sieve of Time: The Memoirs of Leni Riefenstahl*, Quartet, 1992

Samuels, Charles Thomas, *Encountering Directors*, Putnam & Sons, 1972

Schickel, Richard, *The Men Who Made the Movies*, Atheneum, 1975

Seale, Patrick, and Maureen McConville, *Philby: The Long Road to Moscow*, Hamish Hamilton, 1973

Shelden, Michael, *Graham Greene: The Man Within*, William Heinemann, 1994

Sherry, Norman, *The Life of Graham Greene*, 2 vols., Jonathan Cape, 1989, 1994

Vocelka, Karl, *Trümmerjahre Wien 1945–1949*, Jugend und Volk, 1985

Wapshott, Nicholas, *The Man Between: A Biography of Carol Reed*, Chatto & Windus, 1990

Welles, Orson, and Peter Bogdanovich, *This is Orson Welles*, HarperCollins, 1993

Picture Credits